KU-197-725

Fourth Estate

presents

A Mitchell and Webb book:

This

Mitchell and Webb

Book

by

David Mitchell

and

. . .

Robert Webb

Top Tip

Thank you for having bought, borrowed, been given or stolen this book. We want you to get the full value from every single page. So, if there's the slightest chance that you feel you haven't been offered very tremendous value-for-money so far, here's a way to enhance your enjoyment and sense of money well spent (or time well used in borrowing, gift receiving or theft).

Step 1. Go back to the very first page. If you are a slow reader, you may find this a depressing idea, but we promise, it really will be worth it. Go for it!

Step 2. Download the soundtrack to the 'conflicting views on a difficult decision in a nuclear submarine' film, *Crimson Tide*. It's an exciting film, and the soundtrack is very exciting indeed. If you don't own a computer, or don't have the money to purchase the CD, try to become friends with either Denzel Washington or Gene Hackman. These two famous actors starred in *Crimson Tide* and are bound to have a copy of the music. They are known for being nice men as well as terrific actors, and either one of them will at least consider lending you a CD if they value your friendship.

Step 3. Find a quiet place. It's very important that you're not interrupted during Step 4, so find a room and a time where/when you won't be disturbed by you mother/partner/flatmate etc. barging in and asking you what you plan to do about the laundry/Mike's fucking wedding/the fucking earwigs in the fucking cupboard etc. If they do, offer to stab them.

Step 4. Play the soundtrack of *Crimson Tide* on a musical device. Now, hold your copy of *This Mitchell and Webb Book* at arm's length and open it at the very first page. It's quite a heavy book, so you might want to get a friend to help you with this if you have weak arms. This could be because you suffer from an eating disorder due to a sense of worthlessness which may or may not be the fault of your parents. Or it could be that you're a pregnant woman whose muscle tissue has diminished because the hormone relaxin is preparing your pelvis for childbirth. Anyway, with or without the help of a friend, hold the book away from you and then, as you listen to the exciting music from *Crimson Tide*, bring the book gradually closer, turning the title pages as you go. This will give the impression of seeing the opening credits to an exciting film. In particular, it may put you in mind of the film *Crimson Tide* starring Denzel Washington and Gene Hackman.

Step 5. Feel free to read the whole book while listening to the soundtrack from *Crimson Tide*. It will make the whole experience feel much more urgent and worthwhile. In fact, listening to the soundtrack from *Crimson Tide* makes basically anything you do seem more important. Try it while doing the ironing or having a poo. But be warned: the soundtrack to *Crimson Tide* really is very exciting indeed, so, in the above instances, be careful not to burn your fingers or sustain a rectal prolapse.

There! What other book has ever given you such a friendly introduction?

Enjoy!

Acknowledgements

The authors would like to thank everyone at Fourth Estate and at HarperCollins, especially Rupert Murdoch for all his tireless support, late-night chats and dogged proof reading. (But there's still no 'e' in 'glacial' Rupe, you silly old prick!!) Thanks too to Barbara Dixon for bravely stepping in for the photo-shoot on page 196 and to Radiohead for lending us their copy of Microsoft Word. This book could not have been written without the help of all those who taught the authors how to read. Thank you all, we hope you're proud of what you've done. Special thanks go to our editor, Virginia Bottomley, for her patience, wisdom and interesting stories from being in the Major cabinet. (We owe you for all those cheesecakes, Ginny!!!) And last but not least, heartfelt thanks go to our agent, The Doctor (sorry about the crumbs in the TARDIS!) for getting us that massive advance just before the economy went tits-up. Thanks, Doc, you're the best!

To Douglas Hogg, for all the laughter . . .

First published in Great Britain in 2009 by
Fourth Estate
An imprint of HarperCollins*Publishers*
77–85 Fulham Palace Road
London W6 8JB
www.4thestate.co.uk

Visit our authors' blog: www.fifthestate.co.uk

Copyright © David Mitchell and Robert Webb 2009

1 3 5 7 9 10 8 6 4 2

The right of David Mitchell and Robert Webb to be identified as the
authors of this work has been asserted by them in accordance with
the Copyright, Designs and Patents Act 1988

A catalogue record for this book is available from the British Library

ISBN-13 978-0-00-728019-3

All rights reserved. No part of this publication may be reproduced,
transmitted, or stored in a retrieval system, in any form or by any
means, without permission in writing from Fourth Estate.

Designed by Steve Boggs and Nick McFarlane
Printed and bound in Italy by L.E.G.O. SpA – Vicenza

FSC is a non-profit international organisation established to promote the
responsible management of the world's forests. Products carrying the FSC
label are independently certified to assure consumers that they come
from forests that are managed to meet the social, economic and
ecological needs of present and future generations.

Find out more about HarperCollins and the environment at
www.harpercollins.co.uk/green

How to Cope with
Being Normal

Robert Webb

As has become clear to you over the years, every single one of your friends is mad. Perhaps not dangerously mad; maybe it's too soon to spike their drinks with anti-madness drugs or conspire with a doctor to get them sectioned. They probably don't actually scare you or make you question the nature of reality on a regular basis. But still, the evidence has been accumulating for some time now, like hot water percolating through an experience filter to produce a large jug of mad coffee. They are mad. And you are normal. How did this happen?

Before we begin this important scientific investigation, it might be useful to define some terms. By 'mad', I do not of course mean 'genuinely mentally ill'. This is because this is a chapter in a comedy book and 'genuine mental illness' is not usually very funny. If you are a mental health professional or work for a mental health charity, I really can't urge you strongly enough at this point to BACK OFF. Obviously, there is no reason why serious subjects can't be dealt with in a humorous way, but that is not what we're into here and so I do really implore you to SHOVE IT. Similarly, when I use the term 'normal', I'm talking about you. You, holding this book right now, possibly picking your nose, humming the theme tune to a TV show that never existed, standing in Waterstone's, wondering if that guy in the jacket is staring at you, ≫→

hopping discreetly from one leg to the other because you've only just noticed that you need a wee, picturing a child's drawing of a house with blue smoke coming out of the windows . . . you're normal. The blue smoke is drifting upwards out of the windows, not falling out onto the ground like blue dry ice. That would mean you were mad. So, to anyone studying psychology, psychiatry, sociology or any post-structural deconsructionalist semantic doctrine such as hermeneutics or phenomenology, whose reaction to my use of the word 'normal' is something like, 'yeah right, but what does "normal" mean anyway?' I really do in all humility suggest that you PIPE DOWN and SHIT OFF. This is because I, too, am normal. I think I've made a very convincing case.

The madness of your friends is illustrated below.

Now, you may have just noticed a sharp decline in the standard of illustration in *This Mitchell and Webb Book*. This is because the above was drawn by me, rather than by one of our talented designers. As a normal person, I regard anybody who is very good at drawing to be slightly mad. This is normal. Anyway, this particular mad/normal diagram measures your friends across the Uptight/Easy-Going spectrum. I could just as easily have shown a Good/Bad at Art spectrum, where once again I would have been the Normal one in the middle, with the extremes on left and right being labelled Ear-Slicingly Gifted and Unable to Grip a Pencil.

I should also point out here that my ability at drawing is so normal that I've made it look like the maddest people on the spectrum are female, whereas the more moderate three in the centre are male. This is definitely not what I think. If you look closely, you can see that both Languid and Weirdly Detached are sexually ambiguous. I'm not saying that sexual ambiguity is normal (I'm not a student any more) but it's probably more normal than looking like Touchy or Psychotically Brittle.

Interestingly, looking at Touchy, I can't help being reminded of David Mitchell. Perhaps my subconscious was at play when trying to draw someone who looked touchy, and David (for whatever, I mean WHATEVER reason) popped into my head. Does this make me mad? No.

Speaking of David, though, because he is mad, he would probably say that my drawing of Normal is, in fact, far from normal. He probably thinks that my Normal looks to his normal (i.e. mad) eyes unusually relaxed, if not dangerously feckless. And he might think that my Touchy is the most normal-looking one, since he seems to be worried about something and has a sensible parting. There's really nothing much we can do about this madness of his. Except perhaps muse that a comedy double-act where both partners were agreed on what Normal looks like would be rather dull. I won't name names. And one where the partners placed Normal more than one space apart wouldn't last very long. Heard of Bachman and Holness? I thought not.

Perhaps it wouldn't be too mad to apply this humble diagram to the field of political extremism. For example, if we wanted to draw a box that could adequately contain the figure of Adolf Hitler, we would put it to the left of Psychotically Brittle and then just draw the angry ink-splodge made by a broken nib and call it Murderously Resentful. But then we wouldn't be able to say that Hitler's madness was 'off the scale', so let's leave it as it is. To Hitler, being Murderously Resentful was the only normal reaction to the condition of Germany in the 1920s. But he could never have become Chancellor of Germany merely by counting on the support of the Psychotically Brittle. For that he needed the Languid, too. Similarly, you probably need to be a Massive Arsehole to be a member of the British National Party, but only a Dozy Bastard to vote for them.

The way to cope with being normal, then, is to recognize that everyone else thinks that you're mad, but they are wrong. Unless you are Adolf Hitler or Nick Griffin. In which case they have a point.

great flat-share fridge note discourses 1:

darth vader and james bond

Please, James, if you come in late try and be QUIET. Some of us have work, remember!? Darth

NEVER SAY "SUIT ON" THE... HIRE

007

Emperor called again at 8am!!! PLEASE give him your mobile number. He sounds like a cunt. JB

P.S. Please don't leave random things plugged in in the living room.

That was my spare ventilator and IT WAS ON TO CHARGE. Sorry about Emperor –he's got my mobile but is v. old-fashioned about using land lines where possible. Darth

HOME SWEET HOME

007

Have you been drinking my Martini? That bottle was definitely half-full and last night you were in an UNCHARACTERISTICALLY GOOD MOOD. JB

A OK
SHAKE & STIR
Ph- (04) 380 6526

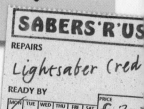

SABERS 'R' US
REPAIRS
Lightsaber (red)
READY BY
MON	TUE	WED	THU	FRI	SAT	PRICE
						£ 24.6

THIS TICKET MUST BE GIVEN UP FOR REPAIRS 6162

Might have had a nip but that's the least you deserve after bumping into your 'friend' - I swear she said her name was 'Loadsa Tits' but that's hardly plausible - in the bathroom using my helmet defluffer as a toothbrush.
    Darth
P.S. Remember to get paper plates for our party tomorrow.

of Pleasure • Pussy Galore's • Emporium of

How come you never use any loo roll? JB

I don't know you nearly well enough to explain that. By the way, it might be handy if you gave me your code-name so I can take work messages when you're out   - Darth

Party great success I thought - shame you couldn't help clear up. M and the Emperor seemed to be getting on very well!   JB
P.S. I don't think you can throw stones name-wise, Darth Vader.

Q called - said 'urgent - don't light any of those cigars.' I expect that explains living room carpet. _ Darth

UNIVERSAL EXPORTS

I'm afraid that's classified.
JB

Is it '007'?
Darth

M v. upset at work today cos Emperor hasn't called her back. Sorry to have to ask but can you give him a nudge?   JB

How the hell did you know that? JB

Not much I can do - like you said, he's a cunt.
        Darth

It's printed on all your stuff.
        Darth

PONTON-BY-THE-WEALTH

Lord and Lady Stockton

are delighted to announce their
12th annual

'CHAMPAGNE & COCAINE EVENING'

Saturday 4th November until the coke runs
out some time on Tuesday morning.

Have your man deliver a simple crossed
cheque for £10,000 to the usual address.

VALET PARKING BY THE HONDA F1 TEAM.

ST PETER'S INTERNATIONAL RELATIONS
DISCUSSION GROUP

Are holding their
weekly Symposium.

Refreshments
from 7pm.
Guest Speaker:
Bill Clinton

VACANCY

A position has opened
up as Lady Stockton's
new Social Secretary.

Salary £140,000 pa

*Please present references from
Roedean School
and the Sorbonne.*

LOST: One Lynx Mk 7 Helicopter

Have you seen this helicopter? Please contact anxious
owner on 03564 387 565. <u>Reward: Life peerage.</u>

ARISH NOTICES

WANTED:

Interpreter to shadow
Polish Housekeeper.
Must be English with fluent
Polish at degree level and
have experience of their
funny little ways.

BELGRAVIA SECURITY ASSOCIATES

Former Special Forces
officer offers discreet
solutions in kidnapping/
ransom scenarios.
Note: I am not a stripper so
please don't ask.

FOR SALE: ISLAND OF TORSA.

Just off NE Scottish coast.
250 acres, population: you.
Bit windy but ideal if you hate other people.

PONTON-BY-THE-WEALTH HUNT

As we all know, some years ago the Ponton-by-the-Wealth Hunt was made illegal by Tony Blair and his rabble of Communist utter bloody shits. But now, with some minor adjustments, we are proud to announce its return.

In an imaginative compromise over land usage, the local Travellers have agreed to scamper over the usual areas next Saturday.

 Paintball guns will be supplied.
Please bring your own Jeep.

Wealthy widow seeks Lawrentian
bit of rough for gardening work and
beaucoup de bonking! Authentic
Nottinghamshire accent preferred
and nice manners a must!
Also, lovely fat cock!

Billionaire international finance
tycoon seeks human affection of any
kind. Please, please someone give me
a hug and kiss it all better.

Be Careful When Doing Something Stupid

H.M.G. HEALTH COMMISSION © 1972

Dear Mr Allen

I was excited to see the adverts on the internet for the BBC's 'Salt of the Sitcom' campaign to encourage working-class people to have a go at writing a sitcom. Some people think that the whole idea is patronising and typical of a BBC desperately casting around for legitimacy and something as good as Only Fools and Horses. I couldn't disagree more and I hope you like my proposal. With your kind permission, it is as follows.

Yours sincerely,

Gorden Ferris

Gorden Ferris
22 Lockheart St,
Leeds.

'You Know Who Your Mates Are'
a sitcom proposal by Gorden Ferris.

Introduction

'You Know Who Your Mates Are' (from now on I'll call it Y.K.W.Y.M.A. as this will be quicker in the long run) is, or hopefully will be (hint hint) a comedy programme about six friends who live in a caravan together and get on well. They all like a pint and sometimes have rows but they sort themselves out, none of them are that bothered most of the time. Sometimes one of them likes to make a fuss but the others tell him to calm down and have a drink and then he's alright. The other thing they have in common is WOMEN. They all have girlfriends most of the time and none of them is queer. Sometimes the people in the next door caravans start taking the piss by saying they are queer but they aren't.

The Characters.

Bob

Bob has dark hair and likes a pint. He is sort of the leader and he can always be relied on to have a bloody good night out on a Friday. He doesn't say much but knows his own mind.

Trevor

Trevor is a bit gobby but is basically alright. He has a brilliant sense of humour and is amazing at remembering jokes. He sometimes gets carried away and says fuck in front of women so Bob has to give him a slap but he soon calms down.

Paul

Paul is built like a brick shit-house but wouldn't hurt a fly. He keeps himself to himself but is always fair. The others sometimes take the piss because he eats so much but he doesn't mind and anyway they know he eats a lot because he's such a big bloke. Paul is a nice bloke but absolutely no use in a fight.

Steve

Steve is shorter than the others and can be a bit annoying. Most of the time he just gets on with it but when he's pissed he can get a bit sarcky. Bob and Paul sometimes have to square him up when he is like this but he is basically alright as long as he's quiet which he generally is.

Richard

Richard doesn't say much but is very sensitive and this means that the women he sleeps with tend to be soft in the head. As well as having more CSE's that the others, he also has three O levels so Trevor is always taking the piss and calling him The Professor.

Jason

Jason is the quiet one. He hardly ever speaks and is a bit of a conundrum.

An Example Programme

Paul and Bob are in the caravan having their dinner. Trevor comes in and starts taking the piss out of Paul for being a fat bastard. Paul doesn't mind too much but Bob tells Trevor to leave it and gives him a warning look. Trevor laughs it off and turns the darts on. They carry on like this for a bit.

Then Steve and Richard come in arguing. They've had an afternoon session in the pub and Steve is pissed and being a bit chippy about Richard's qualifications. Richard tells him to fuck off and Bob agrees, saying that Richard's got nothing to be ashamed of. Trevor joins in, taking the piss out of Steve for being a midget. Steve looks like he might smack Trevor one but Bob gives him a warning look. Instead he takes the piss out of Trevor for being queer because now he's sticking up for Richard all of a sudden (probably some joke about Dicks).

Jason comes in and they more or less ignore him. Trevor says that if anyone is a queer then it's Steve because all the women he shags are taller than him. Steve tells Trevor to fuck off and hits the wall and makes a hole in the chipboard. Bob stands up and tells Trevor to stop winding Steve up because Steve can't take it. Steve is in tears by this stage. Paul says they will need to fix the hole in the chipboard. Steve screams that he (Steve) will end up doing it because he's the only one there who isn't queer. Paul, Richard and Trevor tell Steve to fuck off and to stop crying like a fucking woman. Eventually it gets sorted out and they have a few pints.

Web Access - Microsoft Internet Explorer provided by BBC

Favorites   Tools   Help

Search   Favorites

https://www.outlook.ex2007.BBC   Go   Links

Office Outlook Web Access   Find Someone   Options | Damien Allen ▾ | Log Off
Connected to Microsoft Exchange

Mail   Help

Damien Allen
  Calendar
  Contacts
  Deleted Items
  Drafts
  Inbox (765)
  Junk E-Mail
  Notes
  Outbox
  Sent Items
  Tasks
  Search Folders

Reply   Reply to All   Forward

From Tristram Allen<tristram.allen.7@bbc.co.uk>
To Damien Allen<damien.allen.13@bbc.co.uk>
Subject YKWYMA

Thanks for the attached. Christ. Is this really the best of
the lot? We're supposed to make a fucking pilot.

    From Damien Allen<damien.allen.13@bbc.co.uk>
    To Tristram Allen<tristram.allen.7@bbc.co.uk>
    Subject YKWYMA

    Pretty much, yeah. There was one I quite liked that just
    involved a family sitting around watching 'The Royle Family'
    but I thought that might be a bit arch. Also it was sent by
    someone in Knightsbridge so it might not fit the brief. It's
    not that bad, is it?

From Tristram Allen<tristram.allen.7@bbc.co.uk>
To Damien Allen<damien.allen.13@bbc.co.uk>
Subject YKWYMA

Oh come on, hombre, it sucks a big one. We can't have a bunch
of blokes in a caravan giving each other 'warning looks' for
half an hour. I thought at least we'd get something like
Bread. That was working class wasn't it?

    From Damien Allen<damien.allen.13@bbc.co.uk>
    To Tristram Allen<tristram.allen.7@bbc.co.uk>
    Subject YKWYMA

    Yes but it was written by Carla Lane who's been middle
    class since about 1973. Turns out when you let them do it
    themselves it all gets a bit… rough. We could do it single
    camera with no laugh track and put it on after Newsnight?
    Say it's a comedy/docco/drama hybrid?

From Tristram Allen<tristram.allen.7@bbc.co.uk>
To Damien Allen<damien.allen.13@bbc.co.uk>
Subject YKWYMA

We don't have to broadcast the fucker do we? This is a
disaster.

Mail

Calendar

Contacts

Tasks

Documents

Trusted sites

Damien Allen - Outlook Web Access - Microsoft Internet Explorer provided by BBC

Address: https://www.outlook.ex2007.BBC

Office Outlook Web Access
Connected to Microsoft Exchange

Find Someone | Options | Damien Allen ▾ | Log Off

Mail

- Damien Allen
  - Calendar
  - Contacts
  - Deleted Items
  - Drafts
  - Inbox (765)
  - Junk E-Mail
  - Notes
  - Outbox
  - Sent Items
  - Tasks
  - Search Folders

Reply | Reply to All | Forward

From Damien Allen<damien.allen.13@bbc.co.uk>
To Tristram Allen<tristram.allen.7@bbc.co.uk>
Subject YKWYMA

Look we'll just let this Gorden guy to do the first draft
and then get someone normal to re-write the shit out of it.
Make it funny.

From Tristram Allen<tristram.allen.7@bbc.co.uk>
To Damien Allen<damien.allen.13@bbc.co.uk>
Subject YKWYMA

They'd have to stay anonymous though. That's a tough ask. I
can't think of a writer good enough who's desperate enough
for the work.

From Damien Allen<damien.allen.13@bbc.co.uk>
To Tristram Allen<tristram.allen.7@bbc.co.uk>
Subject YKWYMA

Chris Langham?

From Tristram Allen<tristram.allen.7@bbc.co.uk>
To Damien Allen<damien.allen.13@bbc.co.uk>
Subject YKWYMA

Fuck! Fuck! You're fucking joking! Fuck, that's genius. Do
it!

From Damien Allen<damien.allen.13@bbc.co.uk>
To Tristram Allen<tristram.allen.7@bbc.co.uk>
Subject YKWYMA

Cool. You going round to mum's tonight? She's doing fish-
fingers and arctic roll.

From Tristram Allen<tristram.allen.7@bbc.co.uk>
To Damien Allen<damien.allen.13@bbc.co.uk>
Subject YKWYMA

So retro. See you there.

great flat-share fridge note discourses 2:

paul daniels and martin amis

Martin I was saving that Cottage Pie Thank you for replacing it but it is a different sort. I for one can definitely TASTE THE DIFFERENCE!
Paul

Paul, I enjoyed your ingenious brand-based pun nearly as much as your cottage pie, or 'Cottage Pie' as you call it. That's to say I enjoyed both 'Not a lot'. RE your magician's soirée - I shall be in my room, writing, but sweet of you to ask.

Martin, I didn't ask, as well you know! Last time you got tanked up and called Ali Bongo a 'shit'. Please stay away tonight.
PS. you've done the recycling wrong again.

Paul, Ali Bongo had it coming. He said that London Fields was 'up its own arse' and professed a facile admiration for Beckett. You are too hard re. the recycling. I'm working on my new novel, 'Dread-Schedule Influx - a Fairytale and can't always remember which bottles go in which bins. PS. 'You've done the re-cycling wrong again' is a vicious thing to say to a writer.

Martin, thank you for trying harder with the floor. It is now basically clean. I know you are under a lot of pressure what with never having won that book prize. But please don't be difficult tonight.
IT MIGHT BE MY ONLY CHANCE TO GET DEBBIE BACK

Paul— good party. What was the heavy fuel in the punch? Woke up feeling id-dipped with species shame. Who was the invoice-faced blonde with the corrugated laugh?

Martin, That was my wife. You spent half the night flirting with her and the other half sat in the corner on a beanbag with Derren Brown, taking the piss out of everyone. I'm not talking to you.

Paul, what have you done with my 'The Thorn Birds' mouse-mat? That was an ironic gift from Saul Bellow. You know I can't write without it!

M, You'll get it back when you apologize. The electric and the rates are overdue — they were your job.

Paul, I can't find my mouse-mat anywhere. I suppose you've hidden it in one of your secret compartments. How can I pay the bills if I can't write?

Don't come the pauper with me, Martin. I know full well you've got money left over from that corporate you did for Birdseye.

Paul, That was for a rainy day; AKA the *coming apocalypse*. I must warn you that you have chosen the wrong medium for this confrontation. At the moment I'm just angry. Don't let me become talented. You don't want me to use my talent on you. No… you don't want that at all.

Christ you don't half talk some bloody balls. Why have you started typing?

All novelists acquire a super-mammalian typing speed and besides, I miss *my italics*. Handwriting doesn't agree with my wrist - it starts to creek with marrow-fatigue like the unwilling appendage of some Hungarian mountebank spoon-merchant.

M, If you're having a go at Yuri Geller then maybe we can make up!

Paul, Sorry about Debbie. It's just that she kept saying I was *tall*.

Martin, Yeah that worked on me too.

HOLIDAY IN PLACES THAT

Choose from our range of holiday packages to historic...

CARTHAGE! TROY! ATLANTIS

CARTHAGE:
Pre-AIDS Africa at its best!

Forget dodgy safaris, starvation on the news
and post-colonial hatred and enjoy Africa before
it all went wrong. Do they know it's Christmas?
No, because Christmas hasn't been invented yet!

Yes, the great City of Carthage in the 5th century BC
is the perfect setting for an urban mini-break. Just
soak up the sun and tuck into the food and wine,
safe in the knowledge that, unless you extend your
stay for 1,200 years, you won't meet a Muslim!

TROY:
Geeks bearing gifts!

Our time-travel geeks can transport you to Troy at the
exact moment of its fall to the Greeks. Enjoy a drink
in the Trojan horse head cocktail bar while you watch
thousands of hoplites surge over the ancient city's
walls like maggots on the corpse of a dog!

Be lulled to sleep by the ululations of the Trojan women
or, if you're in energetic mood, have a go on Helen!

**'Finally you'll understand
what the fuss was about!'**
Jeremy Clarkson writing
in *What Minibreak?* magazine

DON'T EXIST ANY MORE!

destinations that have been destroyed including:
HUMBERSIDE!

ATLANTIS:
What's a sunken city like before it sinks!?

It's like anywhere else! Enjoy a relaxing weekend somewhere basically normal where something weird is subsequently going to happen. But not even a special Pizza Express pizza can save this place from sinking!

Quite normal until you start thinking about the impending sinking

HUMBERSIDE:
Kick back and relax in 9th century Humberside!

Ever since Humberside ceased to exist as a non-metro-politan county in April 1996, people have been flocking back there to experience one of the Heath government's most innovative administrative experiments.

But for party-people, check it out in the 9th century, when Friday night was Viking night! Never mind R&R, treat yourself to a bit of R&P (Rape and Pillage) in the way only a weak sun setting over the grey North Sea can make you feel justified in doing!

'There are things you'll find yourself getting up to by the light of a burning hut that you'd never consider in the electric age!' Paul Gascoigne

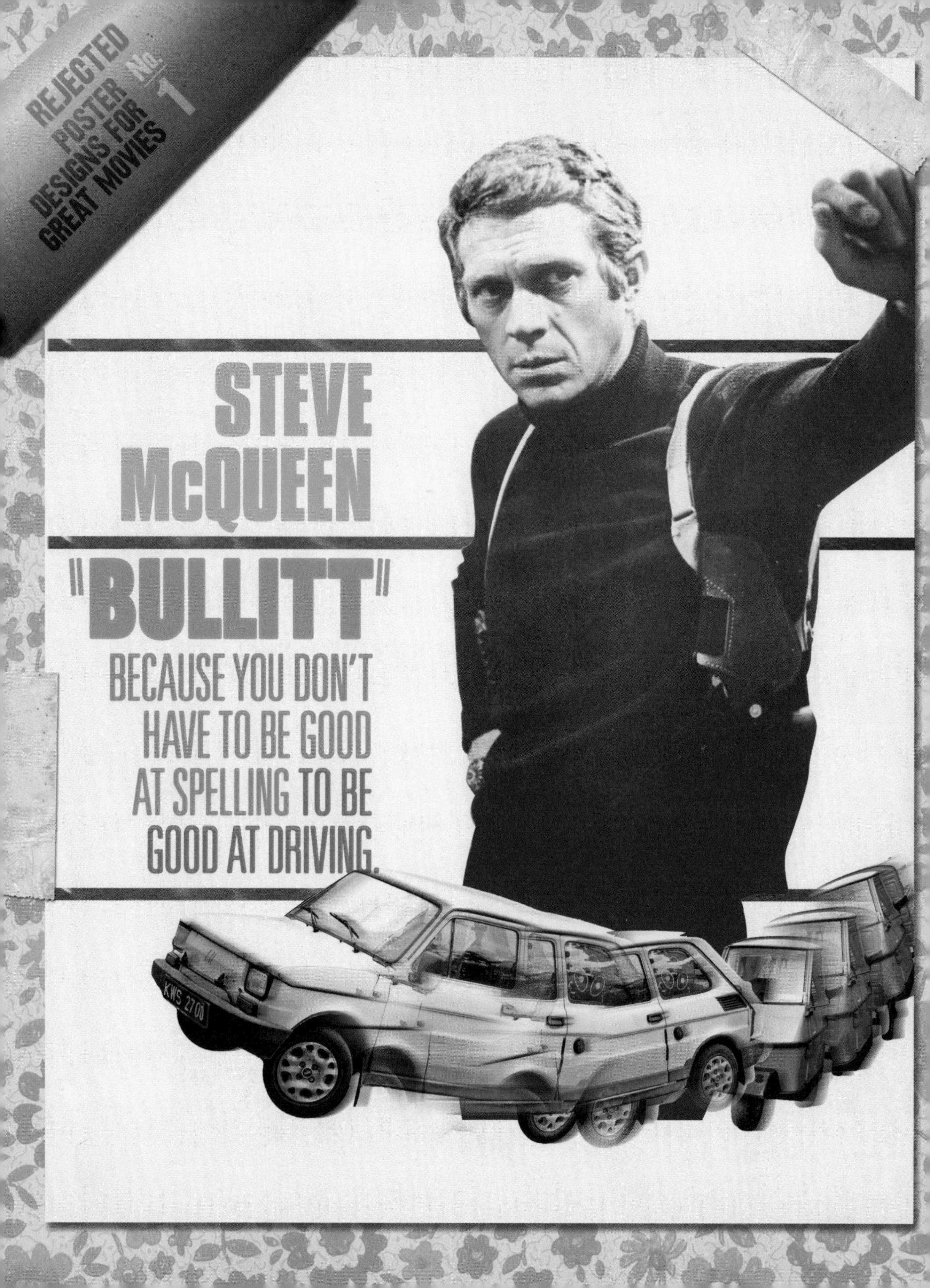

REJECTED POSTER DESIGNS FOR GREAT MOVIES
No. 1
STEVE McQUEEN
"BULLITT"
BECAUSE YOU DON'T HAVE TO BE GOOD AT SPELLING TO BE GOOD AT DRIVING.
KWS 2700

decided that it might not be a good idea. In any event, the standard of ice cream sold in Britain is set to remain high for many years to come. And that can only be good news for all of us. If not for my daughter's teeth! **By Connie Wytcliff.**

Post your comments here

Name (Optional)   **Mail** (will not be published) (required)

Note. Ranting is Free is monitored for abuse and obscenity but not for intelligence, precision, literacy, generosity, sanity, rationality, self-awareness, consistency, wisdom, elegance, courage, honesty or grace.

Submit

updog56
'good news for all of us?' yeah like we all think the same thing obviously? you like ice cream so we all have to. that's great MINE FYOURRER!!!

Forgobin
Perhaps your daughter's teeth wouldn't be in need of dental attention if you spent just a little more time looking after her and a little less time writing your column although it can't take more than 20 minutes because it's rubbish.

umJakelars
'some people have trouble eating ice sream because off sensitive teeth'. Don't make me LOL – I have sensitive teeth and I can hardly eat the stuff. It HURTS when you've got sensitive teetht!!!

Smelgh
Why don't you die? DIE DIE DIE DIE DIE!!!!!!!

RiolandBabel
you put the liiiime in the soda and you drink it aaaall up

Wassup67
You're only writing about ice-cream because you think it will make people like you. Think again. Not that you know how to (think) lol

Poledance3000
Connie Wytcliff? Gitty Halfwit more like!

JonDryTay
It just goes to show you can't be too careful!

Farmland88
One million children a year die of malaria in sub-Saharan Africa alone. And your worried about ice-cream? I don't know how you live with yourself.

BBC BROADCAST FUCK FORM

PLEASE FUCKING NOTE: all producers must fill out one of these fuckers in order to broadcast the word 'fuck' on any fucking BBC network.

Name of Fucking Programme: Last of the summer Wine

Fucking Department: Entertainment, Comedy and Obscure Sport

Fucking Programme Number: 00000000 0000001

Fucking Date of Fucking Transmission: 15th October 1982

Scheduled Time of Fucking Transmission: 5.30pm

Producer's Fucking Name: Bjorn Borg Senior

Reason for use of the fucking word 'fuck' in the fucking programme
(attach separate fucking sheet if really necessary you long-winded fuck):
Compo contracts Tourette's Syndrome from a stale piece of lardy cake

Risk Assessment (who's going to fucking mind and how much):
Lardy Cake manufacturers - loads, fans of Compo - slightly, other viewers - only if woken by offending word

Blamant (who will resign if shit hits fan): Deputy Head of Obscure Sport

Secondary Blamant (who will resign if shit really hits fan): Controller of Filth

Insurance for violence against public by principal artist (who pays up if shit hits fan):
Standard BBC / Prudential Star Spaz plan. NFB. Insurance is invalid unless minibars removed from cast hotel

10

Rex Features

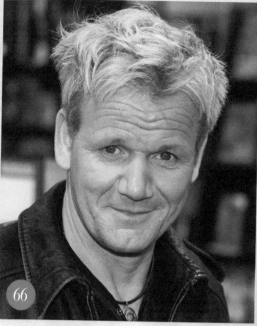

66

Contents

WIN
COLEEN NOLAN'S
BRA!
PAGE 58

Features

10 Cover Story

Why Women are Shit
Psychologist Mark Glee tells us
why we're all a bunch of arseholes.

17 How to Please a Man
Comedian Danny Wallace gives us
his top ten tips on making men happy.

23 Writing Wrongs
In this 10-page special, journalist
Kevin Wilkes argues that there are
too few female writers writing about
womens' issues. **Continued next month.**

34 Out of (eating dis)Order
If your teenage daughter is going to
have an eating disorder, it's best to
be clued up. Anorexia or Bulimia
– which is best? By Derek Man.

Regulars

7 Profile Gok Wan
The style guru has worked tirelessly
for female emancipation by telling
women they've got 'fabulous bangers'.
Why aren't we more grateful?

43 Plastic Surgery Surgery
Your cosmetic surgery
fuck-ups explained.

**56 Make-up, Babies
and Handbags**
The usual.

66 Q&A Gordon Ramsay
The celebrity chef tells us what
underwear he likes in a way
that will definitely give us an
insight into how men think
because this is something
we should definitely
be not just curious
about but basically
obsessed with.

Don't miss the next issue of Observer Woman – out 20 December

Observer Woman Kings Place, 90 York Way, London N1 9GU. T (00) 3361 1000. Email observer.woman@observer.co.uk, www.observer.co.uk/woman. Editor Nicola Jeal Deputy editors Nes Vernon Louise Prance Contributing editor Robert Yates Associate editor David Marcus Creative director Carolyn Roberts Art editor Paul Reed Picture editors Kathryn Greig Williamson (The Observer). Contributors Emily Stokes Mimi Spencer Louise Carpenter Annalisa Monticelli Sarah Katie Phillips Jo Jones Helen Jackson Morgan Myerson. Reproduction CTT Imaging Dept With thanks Leah Jewett Nara Advertising manager Joe Doherty Kalkat

Mitchell and Webb's
Kids Just Don't Know Their Woods

Oak

Perhaps the most normal of the woods, know an oak by its dark colour and its smell of wine.

Hardwood

Hardwood forms naturally into shelving units under tectonic pressure. Harvesting the hardwood is dangerous work, which is why hardwood can be expensive. Learn this.

Pine

Pine is an excellent medicinal wood. Avoid Pine trees when skiing and it will be like you never broke your legs! Pine can be used in any tasty risotto and kills germs fast.

Reslard

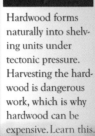

Reslard is a liquid wood and is used as a lovemaking aid by wooden people who've just had an operation. Do not try to drink this wood.

Beech

Beech trees originate from Italy but the wood of a Beech tree is pronounced 'beech', rather than 'el beechio oh-sio'. Learn this to avoid misunderstandings.

Here at Mitchell and Webb we've grown increasingly concerned that young people today just don't know as much about the different sorts of woods as they ought to. Knowing your woods is a vital key to becoming any kind of fully functioning adult, as any adult will tell you. Here is just a glimpse into the fascinating world of different sorts of woods. Once you get hooked, knowing about your different sorts of woods will become an addiction as fun and all-consuming as any lifelong crack habit or fags-jag. Enjoy!

Califonian Redwood

Famously the tallest wood, this wood is actually a mammal. Know the Californian Redwood by the soothing banjo and harmonica noises it emits when being sawn up.

Spargot

Spargot is the only metal wood. The trees were formerly used to link electrical cables but this can now only be seen in parts of Switzerland. Filings of Spargot are used by magicians to perform tricks.

Elm

Elm is an evil wood, hated by everyone. If anyone offers you a chunk of Elm, the only sensible reply is a very firm, 'No Thank You'. For God's sake eschew the Elm.

Pineanium

This is one of the wooden metals. Although there are too many wooden metals to list here, Pineanium is the only one you'll be working with regularly so learn this.

Douglas Fir

Named after the Scottish explorer Douglas Furr, this wood is perhaps the best all-round wood for making cups. Asthma sufferers inject it for kicks.

How to Cope with Pubs

By David Mitchell

There should be no problem coping with pubs. After all, it's a simple idea: they're where we go to make life slow down, to get our daily hit of some chemicals that may very well eventually make it stop. 'Life's too short,' people often say. I'm sure it feels like it, when you're staring death in the face in heart-disease ridden late middle age; when you're regretting all the pints and bacon sandwiches that have clogged your system and made irreplaceable parts of your innards founder. But, even if it is, the evenings, almost anyone must surely admit, are too long. Pubs solve that. They make time go away, without having to watch EastEnders.

This is nothing to be proud of – but it is necessary. That's why pubs were built in such a functional way: counters to buy the booze over and floors that you can easily clean sick off. It was never a trendy thing: there's no reason to be smug that you're there. You're not 'hanging out' or 'being seen'. You get in, nail a pint every half an hour and leave when they chuck you out. Lovely. This is a place that helps you cope, not one you have to cope with.

Until recently. Pubs have changed. They've smartened themselves up. They do food and cocktails. They've got late licences so you can't pace your drinking any more – you're heading for an 11 p.m. finish line and someone moves it two hours further away at the crucial moment. You end up shouting about the editorial policy of the *Daily Mail* and accidentally knocking someone's pint of prawns into their mojito. And some pubs are now restaurants, really. Not labelled as such, but they won't really cope if you sit there next to the knife, fork and tiny dish of rock salt, downing pint after pint of Stella and not ordering so much as a sharing plate of hummus. The pharmacy has gone gastro.

The cumulative effect of the thousands of pubs that have changed in this way on the nervous and sober is incalculable. Suddenly, the moment of walking in is a lifestyle choice, like with a hairdressers or a shoe shop – the very encounters so many of us drink to forget. The stylishness of the menu, furniture and other customers are all intensely threatening. The lighting is so cool, it makes you afraid that it's got a special ultraviolet quality that will reveal the word 'loser' written in semen on your trousers.

Don't misunderstand me, I've never been a fan of the extreme version of the 'old man's pub'. These have always been as frightening to go into as the trendiest gastrobar. Smoky (when that was allowed), sticky with spilt liquor and echoing with emphysema, you're judged just as harshly when you walk into one of those. Ask for a white wine there and you'd better be a woman. At least in trendy pubs, a beer is still as acceptable an order as a cocktail – although you may have to wait 20 minutes for it while the 'mixologist' painstakingly makes cosmopolitans for girls. A perfect opportunity to get talking to them, some might say. Not me – I don't go to pubs to meet new people but to rehearse old opinions with cronies. Going to bars to meet girls is what Americans do (American men. And American lesbians. Amesbians). It seems to make them very happy – that's another reason I need a drink.

I realise I'm now sounding like one of the prejudiced old bastards from the old man's pubs, spouting bile and coughing up phlegm, and I suppose that's where I'll end up. But I'm not ready yet. I realised this in an old man's pub in Kilburn where I, and a few of my friends, had gained a measure of acceptance. The regulars had stopped staring when we came in – and not just because they'd succumbed to cataracts – and the barman even said hello. It was a bit brightly lit but there was always a free seat – indeed ⟫→

> *If the economy is to grow, women as well as men must become alcoholics, just like they have to pretend to like football*

after every winter, a few more. They sold crisps, the lager wasn't cloudy and the roof didn't leak – it was really ticking all the boxes.

But if you went in there on a Saturday, something terrible happened. They had a big screen, presumably installed with a view to becoming a venue for watching sport. Sadly, the Sky contract had long since lapsed, but on a Saturday night, they made use of the screen. Can you guess what they showed?

Seventies porn? No (but please refer to Page 180: *How to Cope with Staying in a Malmaison Hotel*). The speeches of Adolf Hitler? No. A documentary about liver failure? No. All of these would have been preferable. They showed BBC1. On a Saturday night. To people who may not have been painting the town red but were at least 'out'. Who had made some sort of celebratory effort, if only so they could say on Monday morning, in answer to the question, 'What did you do on Saturday night?' something other than, 'I stayed in and watched BBC1'.

However low your expectations from an evening's drinking, they are higher than sitting amongst dying old men, watching *Casualty*. The irony of the title is overwhelming.

Time for the sexist paragraph. Or more sexist paragraph. Most women don't really like pubs. That's why they've gone trendy and foody and cocktaily – to try and tempt women in, against their better judgment. Thousands of pubs have risked alienating their dipsomaniac male heartlands to court the fair weather pre-nightclub female pound. If the economy is to grow, women as well as men must become alcoholics, just like they have to pretend to like football. And the result? Pubs are packed with groups of partying women who'd be equally happy in a wine bar or round each other's houses, and lonely sods like me feel embarrassed they haven't ironed their shirts, and have to wait ages to get served while the barman chops more limes or wipes the sea bass special off the blackboard. The calm of the elephants' graveyard has been disturbed by loads of flamingos on a hen night (or hens on a flamingo night). For more information on my 'Men are Elephants, Women are Flamingos' view of humanity, please see my medical notes.

So, that's the problem as I see it – but how to cope? The only way to counteract the feelings of embarrassment and deracination caused by pubs going cool is to get into real ale. This may sound like an odd weapon with which to fight the forces of fashion, but it works.

Gastropubs, you see, like to think of themselves as returning the pub to how it ought to be – to some golden age when hostelries supposedly weren't just the haunts of liquor and defeat – a Dickensian inn but with access to goat's cheese and the soundtrack from *The Beach*.

So they know they're supposed to do real ale – there's no denying pubs always have. And increasingly real ale has associated itself with so many fashionable buzz-phrases like 'organic' or 'locally sourced'. Without being remotely cool, it answers to the description of a cool thing. And yet, to the young landlord fitting halogen uplighters along the bar, it is a baffling mystery involving pumps and barrels in the basement. You don't just press a button and a pint comes out – you have to yank on a handle several times to produce a liquid which there's every chance that the beardy CAMRA freak who you're trying to please will hold up to the light and pronounce 'off'.

Walk into even the trendiest gastropub behaving like you know about real ale and you will rob the self-regarding management of all their confidence – they'll allow you to taste the ales before buying and watch you sip as if you're the man from Del Monte and John Torode rolled into one. The tables are turned: the mojito buyers are queuing behind you and still the barman is defensively explaining that they 'have the lines cleaned twice as often as the brewery recommends'.

TITANIC

She's OK but
the bloke drowns.

"I've got that thing where I've bitten the
inside of my mouth and so now there's
a bit of a raised bit so I keep doing it."

GENGHIS KHAN

Why Have All The

We're all suffering the effects of lower and lower walls, but why is it happening and what can we do about it? We rang the *Guardian*'s best-paid writers at 4.52 a.m. to see what they thought.

Polly Toynbee
Look at the figures. In their 2009 survey, the ONS carefully charted the height of all walls in areas with a median income which was below, around or above the national average for that area including every other area notwithstanding height or time. The results were chilling. In every case there was a 4.34527% rise or fall in the *[we hung up]*

George Monbiot
Fucking hell. Me and Ben Elton were warning everyone about this in fucking 1987 but did anyone listen? No they fucking didn't. What are we going to do about it?!! You're asking me what are we going to do about it?!! NOTHING! IT'S TOO LATE YOU STUPID BASTARDS! Screw you all — Ben's saved me a place in his rocket.

Max Hastings
Any discussion of this topic will prove fruitless unless our troops are adequately trained and equipped. What is the earthly point of Trident or taller walls when our Marines are expected to engage the enemy with little more than a pea-shooter and a box of Swan Vesta? It's like something out of *Whizzer and Chips*.

John Harris
This is a bit like that pivotal Glastonbury of 1994 when Blur and Oasis were on the same bill but they were still basically getting on with each other. Isn't it? Is it not? Right, well I can't really help then.

Zoe Williams
I'm pregnant again! Can you believe it? Mega! Is it just me or have lots of other women had the experience of being pregnant? Answer? It's just me. This has literally never happened to anyone else and that's why my insights are so valuable. Thank goodness for me.

Andrew Rawnsley
Deep in the bowels of Westminster, the rumble of 'Wallsgate' as I have dubbed it with crushing predictability is beginning to roar and rumble like a piece of toast that David Cameron might have eaten and not digested properly. Hmm, yes, aaaaaaah-haaaaaaa . . .

Walls Got Lower?

Tristram Hunt

It's simply inconceivable that the Victorians would have allowed our walls to fall into such a state of shoddy disrepair. I've got a PhD in this, just about, so I definitely know what I'm talking about because I did several quite good essays on this very subject. Hang on a tick while I dig one out.

Timothy Garton Ash

The key is Europe. The institutions of Europe need to be strengthened through reform if they are to have continued relevance in a changing world. Right, what are we talking about?

Seamus Milne

Sooner or later this is all going to be laid at the door of a certain war criminal. I think we all know to whom I mean. A certain war criminal called Tony. A certain war criminal otherwise known as Mr Tony Blair. Tony Blair the war criminal is to whom I'm referring to lest you may ask. Yes.

"If I know two things, it's that Barack Obama is groovy."

Jonathan Freedland

If I know one thing it's that we shouldn't be too quick to blame Israel. If I know two things, it's that Barack Obama is groovy. You can't possibly expect me to think of a third thing.

Philip French

I was sitting in a cinema in Marseilles in 1907, thinking about films when it occurred that if I was going to spend the next 110 years doing something pointless, I should at least do it well. So much for that!

Mark Lawson

Actually, the issue of low walls has been treated differently across the main soaps, with *EastEnders* accentuating the human cost, with the closure of Clem's wall shop, in contrast to the more light-hearted approach favoured by Corrie. This is interesting.

Simon Jenkins

Here's what we do. Get the walls. Make them taller. If anyone objects – shoot them. If they don't like it, fuck them. Get the wall people and put power directly into their hands. Next, nationalise it. Then privatise it. None of this will work and I'm right. Wubble wubble wubble. See?

LAKEVIEW COTTAGE – VISITOR'S BOOK #4!!

THE BELLAMYS	NOTTINGHAM	15TH – 22ND MARCH
TIM, Ann and baby Jess	HIgh WYCOMbE	22nd – 29th March
Alan and Mary Wonnacott	Chester	29th March – 7th April
Francis and Julia Edwards	Kensal Rise	7th – 14th April
TINA AND JiM SLAVERY	NORWICH	14TH – 21ST APRIL
Eric and Ernay Gash and the boys	Peterborough	21st – 28th April
The Abbotsford Snooker Club	Ormskirk	28th April – 5th May
Andrew Baker's Stag Week!!!		5th – 12th May
The Staplebury Darts League Away Week		12th – 19th May

WE HOPE YOU ENJOY YOUR STAY.

A WONDERFUL COTTAGE WITH DELIGHTFUL WOODLAND WALKS. WILL DEFINITELY RETURN. A BETTER FRYING PAN FOR THE KITCHEN WOULD BE HELPFUL.

A restful week - we spent most of it asleep! Must be the country air.

IT WASN'T THE COUNTRY AIR. IT WAS CARBON MONOXIDE. BOILER BADLY NEEDS REPLACING BUT MARY NOW IN A STABLE CONDITION. I ENJOYED THE WOODLAND WALKS WHILE SHE WAS IN THE OXYGEN TENT.

Well, Alan & Mary, WE think that this is a delightful spot and don't intend to ruin it with a load of TOWNY MOANS!! A little bit of carbon monoxide never hurt anyone and, if you were out having a bracing walk and ENJOYING THE BEAUTIFUL SURROUNDINGS, instead of stuck indoors with the heating on, playing video games I should imagine, then maybe your wife wouldn't be receiving treatment for oxygen deprivation to what, if you ask me, must have been an ALREADY DAMAGED BRAIN!!! Looked everywhere but couldn't find a spaghetti server.

A SPAGHETTI SERVER!? I HOPE I WON'T OFFEND WITH A LITTLE PLAYFUL HYPERBOLE BUT SOME PEOPLE DESERVE TO BE STABBED IN THE EYE WITH A SHARPENED DICK! SHOWER CURTAIN NEEDS REPLACING.

Excuse me for bringing a bit of perspective to proceedings but some people are gay!! (I mean this in the modern sense naff rather than the archaic sense happy/jolly or the subsequent sense homosexual but I would like to register equal disdain for all of these things.) Who needs a shower curtain unless they hate their body!? We've all been parading the woods completely naked looking for shallow graves or morsels of porn. Found a rotting dog! Thought it was a badger for a glorious moment but it turned out to be a dog. But then badgers are so shy.

No snooker table. Looked everywhere.

A quiet week spent writing poetry and contemplating love. Couldn't find recycling bins so have left dead prostitute in airing cupboard.

Found snooker table but no darts board. Woodland walks tiring.

How to Cope with Being Dumped

Part One: Denial and Despair

Robert Webb

Firstly, try to remember that suicide is only a short-term solution. It might have a few superficial things going for it, but looking further ahead, the rewards are really quite limited. I'm not saying that everyone who commits suicide is a loser, but losing seems to be quite a big part of it. To start with, you need to decide that you've lost, then you remember the phrase, 'it isn't the winning that counts, it's the taking part' and conclude that the only way to win ever again is never again to take part; i.e. to lose, lose pre-emptively, lose emphatically and irreversibly, turn your friends and family into losers and, having finally lost it, become lost. And yet you never hear this at the funerals of people who killed themselves: 'What a great sport! He really, really, really didn't mind losing.' No, that's not what you tend to hear.

So having made the only sane decision, life already starts to look comparatively rosy. I've been dumped several times and the worst times were about as much fun as spending three months vomiting turds. Of course, it's not always like that. Sometimes a person might want to get out of a relationship but not have the heart/balls/anus to do the dumping themselves and so embark on a long campaign of passive-aggression and neglect in the hope that their partner will eventually tell them to fuck off. For these people, being dumped is – and this is the last poo metaphor – a genuine relief. So this chapter isn't really for them; they've got what they wanted and can look forward to meeting someone new and not having their friends gossip about how badly they're behaving anymore. No, this is for the real dumpees, the ones who loved and lost, the ones who didn't see it coming, the ones who wander round for weeks looking bewildered and punch-drunk, or just drunk. Welcome, friend. Close the door and for God's sake blow your nose. We are the dumpees and we are legion.

The first stage is, of course, Denial. I cannot advise you strongly enough to get through this stage as quickly as possible. The longer it goes on, the more the person who dumped you will think you're a tit. This will help them justify the original dumping and will have the effect of making them feel better about themselves, which is of course the last thing you want them to feel. A typically bad idea during the denial stage is to write them a letter or email. Actually there will usually be two. The first is the Win Them Back letter, which will be mawkish, nostalgic, embarrassing and doomed. It will be so pathetically self-abasing that the dumper will have to say something vaguely kind in response. You will then, of course, seize on this as evidence of their enduring love and start to tell them that they're confused, they don't know what they're doing and they've put you through all this anguish for no reason. This will make up the body of the second letter, the one called I Just Want You To Know How It Feels For Me, which will be aggressive, pedantic, patronising and, again, doomed. This will at least have the benefit of provoking such a furious response that you will be left in no doubt that you are now single. Congratulations. You can now move out of Denial and into Despair.

Depending what sort of person you are, how much you adored the other person, whether they immediately go out with someone else and what you were supposed to have done wrong in the fist place, Despair will last either a couple of hours or about a year. I'm also open to the idea that it may last any amount of time outside those parameters and will also depend on any number of factors not mentioned. I hope this is helping. ⟫→

What is certain is that Despair is the stage where you find out whether your friends actually like you. Unless you've been a complete tool your whole life, you'll generally be quite chuffed with results here. Your friends will make quite a big fuss of you, buy you drinks, call a temporary halt to doing amusing impressions of you and maybe even forgive you for that time you didn't go to their birthday party because you couldn't be arsed. People will start saying things like, 'if you need to talk, then you know where I am'.

Now, I've tried to avoid gender distinctions so far, but your reaction to the offer of 'a talk' might depend on whether you're male or female. Convention has it that women love talking about their feelings and men would rather suffer in silence. This is largely bollocks. And if you're a gay man or woman, then you've already rejected quite a big convention, so I'm certainly not about to make crazy generalisations about you. But I suppose it's true to say that if you're a straight chap, then getting drunk and blubbing all over your mates is something that they won't mind the first time. They might even feel quite touched and give you a hug. After that, though, be warned. Male, female, gay or straight, nobody likes a miserable bastard forever. They just get bored.

Apart, that is, from Those People Who Live For Other People. You might have come across them: 'Oh God, I'd better go round and take Jane another cake. She's so screwed-up by the way Gary's treated her that she's been literally pissing the bed every night. I'd better go round and offer to change her sheets for her. My hands literally smell of her piss. Here, smell!' These are the people who might mark you down as a 'sad case' or a 'project'. Avoid these ghouls. They are considerably more fucked-up than you and need you to stay in Despair. If they've already stuck their proboscis in then it will be harder to get better, but once you do, they'll soon move on to another host. Possibly you are one of these people, in which case you are beyond my amateur care. Seek proper help or become a bad playwright.

However long you're in Despair, it's also vital that you avoid your Last Boyfriend/Girlfriend But One. If the person that you were going out with before you went out with the person who dumped you is still around or in touch, they may not be able to resist an overwhelming desire to come and rub it in. If *you* dumped *them* then they've come to gloat. If *they* dumped *you* then they've come to reiterate what's wrong with you and discuss your problem with men/women/commitment/ sheep etc. I'm sorry to be harsh about this: anyone sensible in their position would keep a discreet distance. If they suddenly turn up, they're bad news and an arse. Avoid them by pretending to have gone mad. You may indeed have temporarily gone a bit mad anyway: i.e. making playlists of the special songs shared by you and the dumper and playing it endlessly; fetishizing a jumper or bra that they left behind; becoming a mental new enthusiast for Zoroastrianism, etc., but you can always exaggerate if necessary.

So that's it for now: never chase a dumper, let your friends help but don't bore them brainless, avoid wankers bearing gifts.

To be continued . . .

✤

**Disgraceful Things
You Can Learn
from the Internet
No. 403:
How to stab
the Queen**

http://www.stabqueen.org

FAQs: So now I'm ready to sta

In order to stab the Queen, you'll need the following gear:

1. A knife or dagger

2. Access to the Queen

The first item can be sourced at any hardware or kitchen supplies store (suckers!) but for the second you can.

Either: approach her on royal walkabout (maybe when she's opening a hospital or school). This may involve disguising yourself as a little old lady or child (unless you're a little old lady or child – I'm not being prejudiced unlike the Queen I expect!) and hiding the knife in some flowers. This will make it look like you're stabbing the Queen with some flowers which will be comical until the Queen dies (hooray!).

Or: Get an MBE. This is probably the easiest way of getting access to her as to qualify for one you only need like a bronze in the Commonwealth Games or to have helped out at a Community Centre for about thirty years.

FAQs: I've heard the Queen is virtually invincible. Where should I stab her?

<< 1 2 3 >>

PRIVACY POLICY I CONTACT US I TERMS & CONDITIONS

...e Queen. What will I need?

It's true that the Queen is virtually invincible, particularly if you stab her on the hat or 'Crown'. Here's a diagram of where best to stab her:

Her Crown: Don't bother stabbing her here – it's actually metal.

Her eye: Definitely the best and safest place to stab the Queen as even staunch royalists admit.

Her stomach: Probably quite a good place to stab the Queen unless she is currently gestating an alien baby (usually when there's an 'r' in the month) in which case it will cause it to leap out and dissolve you.

Her knee: This will only be a glancing blow and will leave you vulnerable to attack from corgis.

> *BEST OF LUCK*
> *STABBING*
> *THE QUEEN!*

Bob Holness Quotes

Smells

Liz

Celeb dogging

Trash

STOP GOING BALD NOW!

Regency De Montfort Hair and Tricology Systems Clinic™ has an established reputation amongst nearly everyone who works there as Europe's leading and premier baldness hospital.

For just £29,000 we will enrol you in our unique Slapeaze™ program of follicle energization and baldness reductionment which will leave you free to live your life with total confidence that you're throwing money at this problem, whatever your level of hair bereavent and whatever the results.[1]

And what is more, we're conveniently located in London's prestigious Amersham area, so hardly anyone that you know will see you entering or leaving the premises.

BEFORE

AFTER

Each one of our experts has been perfectly measured to fit their white lab coat and is fully trained in all aspects of credit card transactions. So why not pay us a visit and a large amount of money and let us do the worrying for you? You've got nothing to lose except even more hair.

OUR SLAPEAZE™ SYSTEM INCLUDES:

➡ Getting a mirror and angling it so you can see just how very bald you are.

➡ Giving you a despairing look as we say something like, 'Christ, you really are going very bald, aren't you?'

➡ Shining various coloured lights at your baldness. One of these lights may well turn out to be some kind of laser. Cool!

➡ Offering a course of expert counselling called, 'Why Bald People Look Worse than Normal People'. Free tissues.

➡ Selling you what our experts have come to refer to as 'a fucking expensive bottle of shampoo' containing various ingredients which clinical trials have shown to contain ingredients.

Call 0773 664-26976
or go to www.thinkhairythoughtsandhandoverthecash.co.uk

[1] Results may include continued baldness.

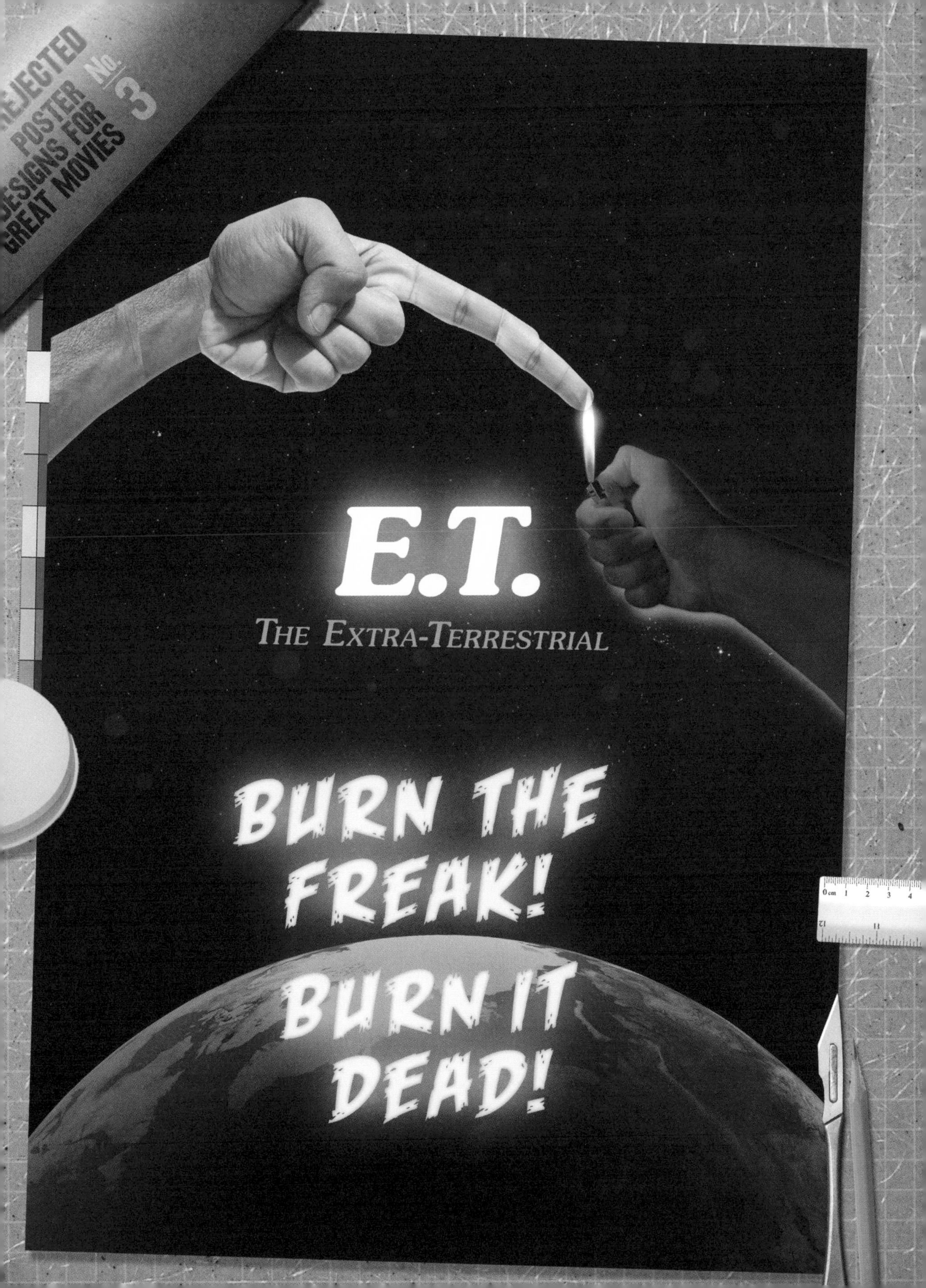
REJECTED POSTER DESIGNS FOR GREAT MOVIES
No. 3
E.T.
THE EXTRA-TERRESTRIAL
BURN THE FREAK!
BURN IT DEAD!

Captain Todger

Captain Todger is Britain's leading Super-Hero. He has saved humanity many times, most recently in his defeat of Professor Malcontent by doing a lethal fart in his lunchbox. Undeniably popular, his public statements have variously been called 'childish', 'reactionary' and 'basically racist'.

What is your idea of perfect happiness?
Lying in a hammock, having a whisky, wanking.

What is your greatest fear?
That my bell-end might come off and fall on the floor.

Which living person do you most admire and why?
Seb Coe. A wonderful ambassador for sport with sound politics and a good haircut. He's an absolute fucking dreamboat.

What is the trait you most deplore in yourself?
I've been racking my brains over this one and I can't think of anything. I'm sorry if that's not good enough for your nancy-boy *Guardian* readers but it's true and that's that so you can get screwed.

What is the trait you most deplore in others?
Intolerance.

What has been your most embarrassing moment?
I don't think I've ever been embarrassed but letting one off whilst I was standing next to a kiddie in a wheelchair was not a good moment. That and 9/11.

What is your greatest extravagance?
I successfully cloned Shirley Bassey and have eight of them at home. They perform various domestic duties but I have never pushed my advantage sexually-speaking, as she is a lady.

What is your most treasured possession?
My penis.

Where would you like to live?
I spend as much time as I can in Gibraltar because it's just basically got everything. Whether you're after nice English food, friendly English pubs or just normal English people, Gibraltar's got the lot.

What makes you depressed?
I have never been depressed. Ever.

What do you most dislike about your appearance?
I have never disliked anything about my appearance. Ever.

Who would play you in a movie of your life?
Peter Egan.

What is your most unappealing habit?
Because I am a Super-Hero, I was born with the ability to lick my own balls. I understand now that it's not appropriate to do this in company. In fact, Her Majesty was highly diverted! She was though.

What is your favourite smell?
My own balls.

What is your favourite word?
Balls.

What is your favourite book?
A Year in Provence by Peter Mayle. Magical.

Is it better to give or to receive?
Errrrrrrrrrrrr! Seriously though, errrrrrrrrr! No. Errrrrrrrrrrr!

What do you owe your parents?
I sprang fully-formed from the loins of King Blabton IX, ruler of the Sblabtons (basically space jellyfish) so I don't know. I don't bother him and he doesn't bother me. We don't talk. Capeesh?

Which living person do you most despise and why?
The comic actor, Craig Cash. I simply cannot see the appeal.

Have you ever said 'I love you' without meaning it?
Yes, but I said it in a very sarcastic voice so at least the lady knew I didn't mean it.

Which words or phrases do you most overuse?
'This is a poignant reversal indeed, Lord Titquiss'. Joking – probably 'arse'.

How would you like to be remembered?
Lying in a hammock, having a whisky, wanking.

DAVID STARKEY'S
COMPLETE HISTORY
of ENGLAND
(1485-1603)

David Starkey is rightly acclaimed as the third or possibly second best historian on British TV. Here for the first time are all his major works, collected into a single box set, showing the full sweep and diversity of Starkey's much-needed contribution. Concentrating mainly on the Tudors, seldom has an historian written so much about such an important, albeit shortish, period in the history of our country, or 'realm' as he would call it.

Titles include:

**SIX WIVES:
THE QUEENS
OF HENRY VIII**
*An account of the six
wives of this famous
Tudor King*

ELIZABETH
*An account of this
famous Tudor Queen*

**THE REIGN
OF HENRY VIII:
PERSONALITIES
AND POLITICS**
More Tudor stuff

**HENRY VIII: MAN
AND MONARCH**
*Another look at this
famous Tudor King*

**RIVALS IN POWER
— LIVES AND LETTERS
OF THE GREAT
TUDOR DYNASTIES**
Some Tudors

**REVOLUTION REASSESSED:
REVISIONS IN THE HISTORY
OF TUDOR ADMINISTRATION
AND GOVERNMENT**
Tudory

**THE ENGLISH COURT:
FROM THE WARS OF
THE ROSES TO THE
CIVIL WAR**
This may include Tudors

Unbeatable value! Buy the David Starkey Complete History
of England [1485-1603] today and we'll throw in a DVD of
David Starkey's major TV series, 'The Tudors' [series one].

HELP THE THICK

Help those for whom every day is a bit of a struggle
(but not so much as would normally be worthy of sympathy)

Ken is just an ordinary guy. By which we mean, he's *just* an ordinary guy. He limped over the line into normality, mental and physical competence. He's not mentally subnormal – not *quite*. He's not physically disabled – but *nearly*. He does knock a lot of things over.

Ken and people like him are the forgotten victims of our society: they're not quite unfortunate enough to qualify for charitable or government help.

For decades people like Ken – who's only a couple of hefty bumps on the head short of a lifetime's cushy spoonfeeding – have been left to fend for themselves. 'They're fine,' society says. 'They may be incompetent, ham-fisted, eye-wateringly unwise – but not quite enough to make it medical.'

People call Ken names: 'spaz', 'moron', 'malco', 'useless nutter' but his tragedy is that he's not quite any of these things – because if he were, he'd get funding. Instead he's left to fend for himself, prey to online roulette, pyramid schemes and those catalogues that try to make you pay for next Christmas in January.

That's where we at *Justice for the Just OKs* (or 'JOKes for short) come in. We try and give help and support to these 'jokes' who would otherwise be left to look after themselves until they became 'beyond a joke' and therefore eligible for state aid.

_____

Please give generously.

And a quarter of our revenue goes to our sister charity, *Victims of Untragic Death* which provides support to the families of people who die marginally too old for it to be deemed particularly tragic – you know, 64, something like that. You still feel hard done by but you can't *particularly* complain.

✝ Victims of Untragic Death®

"Have you noticed that it's always really windy near tall buildings? Why is that?"

GEORGE ORWELL

REJECTED POSTER DESIGNS FOR GREAT MOVIES
No. 4
BASIC INSTINCT
It's definitely her muff.

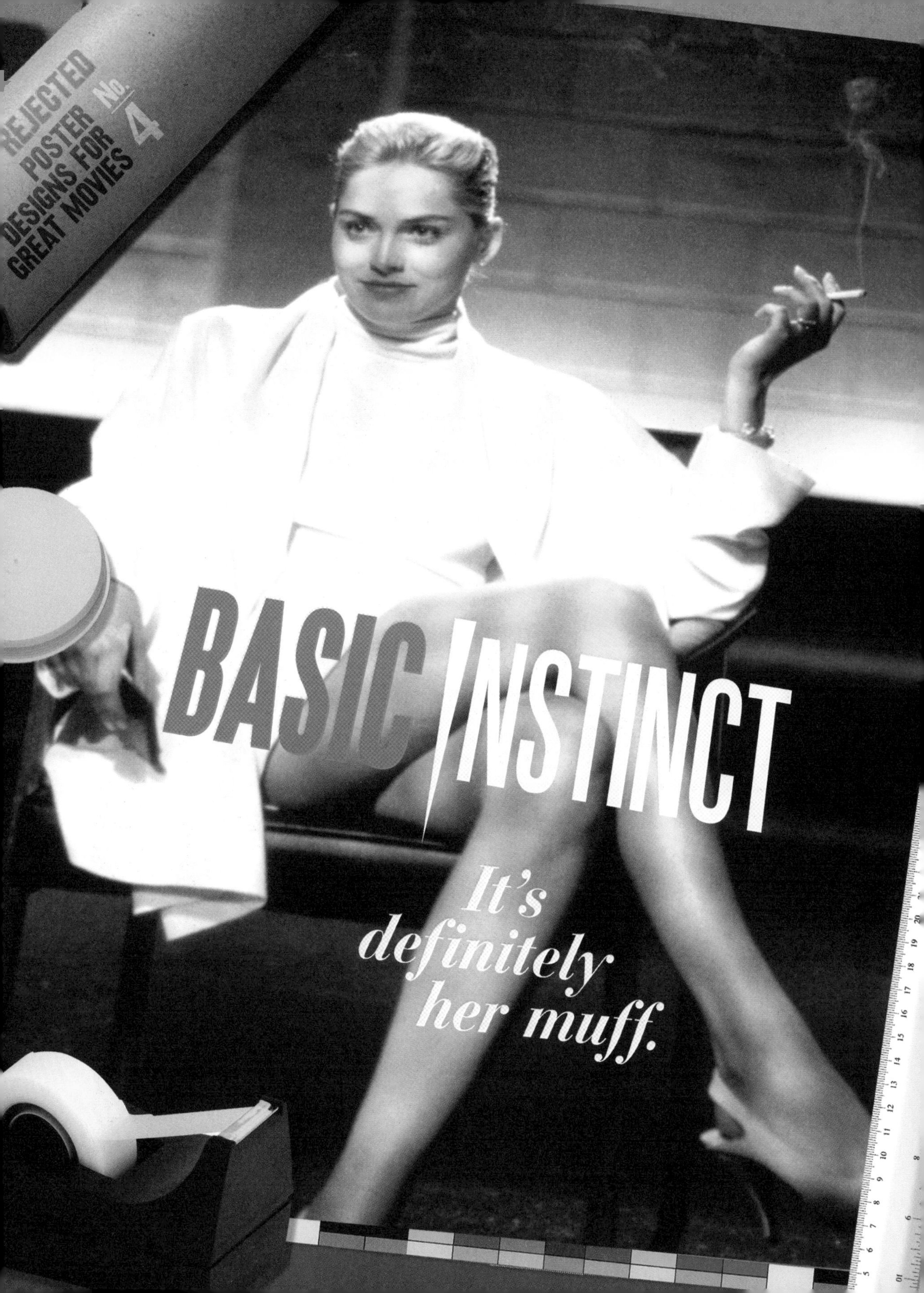

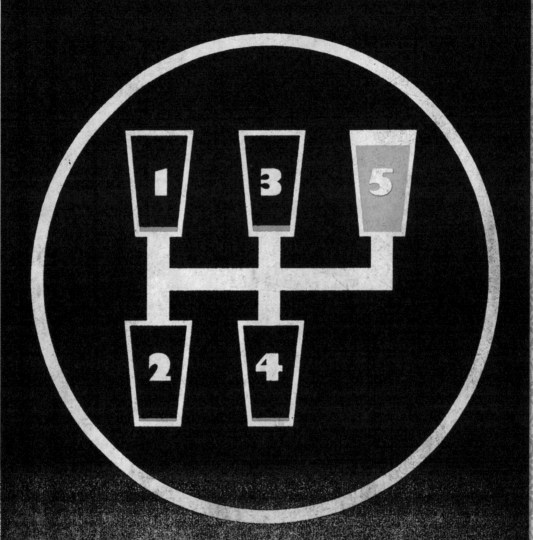

Lucky people live longer – Official

NORWICH Researchers at the Publicity Department of Ray Winstone University, Norwich have found a startling link between human longevity and good luck. In an unprecedented survey, the research team detected a positive link between people who were wealthy, enjoyed excellent heath, lived in prosperous areas of the country, had satisfying and secure work and personal lives and people who described themselves as 'lucky'. The team then went on to apply these high levels of 'luck' to the relative longevity of those surveyed, compared with other sections of society, tagged 'everyone else' and reached the unanswerable conclusion that lucky people live longer.

Among those found to be lucky were various subsets, such as people over 90 and soldiers returning from a recent tour of Afghanistan, both of whom tended to describe themselves as 'lucky to be alive'.

Chief Researcher Kevin Plaster said, 'It's certainly some kind of breakthrough. We've always intuitively assumed that lucky people are lucky, but now it's a scientific fact.

'We haven't been able to establish if people live longer because they're lucky or if it's just that lucky people live longer. For that we're going to need another grant of at least £200,000. That's vital for this important work to continue.'

Plaster is the author of several other studies in the field of sociological phenomena. Among his work most celebrated by randomly assigned newspaper science editors is his discovery that 'Smiling Makes You Look Happy' and also that 'People With No Legs Do Less Walking'.

LONDON PAPER

As he prepares to go into the I'm a Celebrity Jungle, Dr Jonathan Miller talks for twenty seconds to our celebrity editor, Ariadne Pasteur, about his philosophy of life, how to direct live opera and other things to fill up the twenty seconds.

What's your definition of a great night out?
Unfamiliar as I am with many of the late night 'boites' that are frequented–

Describe a nightmare date.
Well, it's been many years since–

People describe you as a sex symbol. Why?
Gratifying though it always is to–

You're a doctor. What are your skincare tips?
In an age where we seem increasingly obsessed by–

You like opera. What's good about it?
How can one attempt to express the–

Why do you think it is that old people die so soon?
Surely what you mean to say is that–

Thank you very much Dr M!

NEXT WEEK A.C. Grayling!

Alan Bennett

'He really ... dishes the shit ...

I BEGGA YOUR PARDON SIGNORETTA!?

Is it me or does no-one speak English any more?

I was having a traditional English burger and fries in a café near me and couldn't get the waitress (or maybe that should be waiter if I don't want to get arrested by the sexism police) to understand the simple word 'ketchup'. The miserable slav-faced fat little madam just gawped at me as if I'd asked her to recite the names of all the Kings of Poland, which she'd probably be able to do anyway as she's no doubt got a PhD in History from the Polish University of Concentration Camp! I don't hate foreigners nearly as much as people say I do but is it really too much to expect that she might have mugged up on the names of the major sauces while she was on the raft heading over here or however the hell these parasites travel!? In the end I had to ask for the ketchup again before she gave it to me. On the plus side, she was up for paid sex. No prizes for guessing who paid! Me!

Try looking it up!

GET YOUR FAT ARSES OFF OUR BEN-£-FITS JOHNNY FOREIGNER!

If I lived in a horrible sweaty country with spicy food and no freedom, I'd probably want to come to Britain to luxuriate in a B&B, care of the council, and spend my social security on rum and ganja too. I've got nothing against them. But why don't they try to get jobs!? They could work in cafés or something. That way at least they'd be making an effort to integrate into our society rather than just hanging around, breathing our air while they worship their strange gods and play their awful music.

CHEESE IS MADE BY ALIENS

That got your attention. But it isn't. The congestion charge should be stopped, thoug[h]

QUE?

NEW LABOUR? NEW C***S MORE LIKE!

❑ We are Labouring (yes!) under the most evil government since the Nazis. These guys are psychos and want us all dead as has been made clear by all the things they've done and the evidence. What more proof does anyone need!? People don't often get burned to death these days but I'm sure I'm not the only one who thinks that the spectacle of the entire cabinet being burned alive, screaming and finally, irrelevantly, penitent, would be cheering and much more entertaining than most of the muck on the BBC. Or, to keep it carbon neutral (so you can stand down, PC P.C.), let's smother them. Yes, smother them. Smother them, smother them, smother them. Just like they've smothered us, but less metaphorical. I want to feel the point when the life in their eyes blinks out, when they stop struggling, my Shipman moment.

WHY AREN'T THEY CATCHING THE REAL CRIMINALS?

Does anyone like speed cameras, apart from lesbians? Why can't we drive as fast as we like? If God had meant us to drive slowly, he wouldn't have created gas pedals and plenty of children so it's not the end of the world if you hit a few. And yet the cameras are everywhere, snooping on the likes of you and me when they could be catching rapists. If the lesbians hate rape as much as they claim, why don't they campaign to have speed cameras converted into rape cameras!? And the footage could be sold to kinky internet sites – it would all pay for itself!

PRISONS STUFFED TO BURPING POINT?

L imp-wristed bureaucrats are always telling us how overcrowded our prisons are, as if that's an excuse for sentencing serial child murderers to go on a free holiday and have 'a long hard think about what they've done'. At the same time, we tax-payers have to stump up to feed and clothe the hundreds of thousands of total shits staying at Her Majesty's pleasure. Well I say, turn off the food hose. Problem solved! They'll eat each other! This will save law-abiding citizens money and keep prison numbers down. And it'll put a stop to all this 'letting them out after a while' nonsense. Even a couple of months in a cannibalistic hell-hole will turn even minor criminals into either savages or sandwiches. Either way, there's no possibility of their being reintegrated into society. Phew!

* The lawyer wishes us to point out that this page isn't really by Alan Bennett. Obviously, anyone who thought it was has utterly missed the point.

GRAND TEMPLE OF THE HOLY EYE OF THE STORM OF VECTRON'S DREADFUL LOVE

Welcome to the celebration of the bonding commitment made by:

ASPIRATIANA BASKERVILLIOR-ZAPP
(FEMALE, SLAZZBAT 7)

To

ERIC KNOWLES
(MALE, EARTH)

'May their love be as tangible as Vectron's beard, as fragrant as Vectron's breath and as long-lasting as Vectron's erections (or Erectrons).'

CHAPTER 90, VERSE 0 OF THE FIFTH LOST SCROLL OF VECTRON.

PRESIDING: Grand High Bishop Excelsior McGill, supplicant to Vectron's mighty learning curve, and Tim Wonnacott from Bargain Hunt.

ORDER OF SERVICE:

PRAYERS TO VECTRON: the Grand High Bishop will lead the congregation in the Great Introductory Hello Prayer which Vectron sent down to us hidden inside a meteor(ite):

BISHOP: I am the Lord Vectron!

ALL: You are the Lord Vectron!

BISHOP: I am all that is Goodness and Gracious.

ALL: Me.

BISHOP: Bow down, all those who would be spared!

ALL: What?

BISHOP: (Explosion noises – use microphone)

ALL: We asked for that!

BISHOP: Let all be peaceful in the galaxy and the dark sky but a soft velvet curtain set with the brightest jewels.

ALL: Until you get close and realise it's all rocks and gaps.

BISHOP: Praise Vectron!

ALL: Pardon?

BISHOP: (Louder – use microphone) Praise Vectron!

ALL: Oh.

FIRST READING: Tim Wonnacott of Bargain Hunt will read a personal message from Michael Parkinson reminiscing about his years working with Eric Knowles on Going for a Song and congratulating him on marrying an alien (or alion).

HYMN 26,787 IN 456,752 VECTRONIC HYMNS FOR TODAY: Heehoowoo Devalleyan Bee (Gay Nstalldy Zasta)

PRAISE VECTRON: the congregation will praise Vectron in the manner that Vectron himself taught us (or tortoise). Goggles recommended.

SECOND READING: Nondescriptiana Baskervillior-Zapp (the mother of the bride) will read an extract from Ten Things I Love About Vectron by Philip Larkin.

SERMON: Grand High Bishop Excelsior McGill will prepare the couple for their life together with a selection of his edgy racist jokes.

THE MARRIAGE: the Bishop and Tim Wonnacott of Bargain Hunt will conduct the full official Vectronic Bonding Ceremony (non-sex version).

THE SIGNING OF THE REGISTER: this will be done using lasers for reasons of time. Goggles recommended.

THE VALUATION OF THE ANTIQUES: your chance to make use of the renowned expertise of both Eric Knowles and Tim Wonnacott of Bargain Hunt .

HYMN 324,987 IN THE ALL NEW VECTRONIC SONGBOOK: 'Don't Take the Love of Vectron into the Bath or You'll Set Fire to the Water!'

THIRD READING: Philip Serrell and David Barby, also from Bargain Hunt, will read the lyrics from some Flanders and Swann songs as if they're in some way moving. Goggles recommended.

COLLECTION: all money received will go towards the 'Intergalactic Fund for the Discovery of Who Vectron Is'.

PLEASE STAND AS THE HAPPY COUPLE LEAVE.

RECESSIONAL: The Imperial March from The Empire Strikes Back but sung to the word 'Vectron'. The congregation are respectfully asked to try this at home first.

David Mitchell and the Meaning of a Bad Back
– a 1 hour documentary for BBC2

Following the success of Stephen Fry's investigation of Bi-Polar Disorder and Gryff Rhys Jones' programme about anger, RedBurp Productions are developing a ground-breaking documentary which will be along the lines of the same sort of thing.

Everyone knows that David Mitchell is a successful comedy writer/performer and the rightful successor to Ned Sherrin. What many people DON'T know about him however is that he suffers from sciatica: a chronic back problem commonly known as 'having a bad back'.

Over the course of the documentary David will:

- TALK movingly to camera about how his back sometimes hurts

- TAKE us on a visit to his chiropractor, telling us that he has no idea whether this does any good but you'd feel a fool for not doing anything

- MEET fellow celebrity bad-back sufferers such as, say, Jordan and offer her an 'imaginary red button' which could take her bad back away but would also take away all the positive effects of having a bad back such as providing an excuse for getting out of doing anything you don't want to do. The viewers will be intrigued by Jordan's response to this

- DISCUSS how having a bad back is a modern taboo. If it turns out that having a bad back is NOT a modern taboo then we can drop this bit because there's such a load of great other stuff – see above

We think you'll agree with us that this is all excellent.

And we've saved the best news till last. David Mitchell himself is fully committed to the project, saying, and we quote his agent, that he is 'basically up for it as long as the money's right'.

So it's over to you guys at the BBC to get your thinking caps on over this no-brainer.
The proposed budget breaks down as follows:

RedBurp administration costs	£4m
David Mitchell's fee:	£75,000ish
Catering:	£400
Additional production costs, cameras, crew etc:	£1000?
Contingency:	£50
Total:	**£4,076,450**

We hope you agree that this provides unparalleled value for money for BBC viewers.
Finally, below are some alternative titles.

- *'David Mitchell's Imaginary Red Button'*

- *'(Bad) Back to the Futon with David Mitchell'*

Only to be used in the event that we focus on how a bad back can lead to mental breakdown and redundancy:

- *'David Mitchell – Back, Sack and Crack'**

*if we're going to be on BBC3.

"Yeah, Ocado are pretty good I must say because they actually have delivery windows of only an hour which is handy."

HAROLD PINTER

The British press are famed the world over for the hilarious puns in their headlines, but this level of excellence isn't achieved by accident. It's achieved on purpose. And, more than that, it's not the sort of 'on purpose' you'd expect. The days of waiting for a news story to break and then thinking of a punning headline that was appropriate to it are far behind us. A demanding 21st century readership means that hilarity must be approached scientifically. The very best comedy writers in the world have been recruited to create, in advance, a punning headline for almost any eventuality. So, when the news story breaks, the headline is already there. We have been given a privileged glimpse into the archives of the country's foremost news gathering institutions in order to bring you just a few examples of the hilarious headlines waiting for reality to catch up.

You're the Wan that I Won't!

To be used in the event of Gok Wan being turned down for sex by someone deemed promiscuous.

LOCATION..............................
DATE..............................

PROJECT FROM THIS SIDE
ARROW SHOWS POSITION

A Real Burn-up for the Tooks

To be used in the event of the house of the family of the late humourist and broadcaster Barry Took being destroyed by fire.

LOCATION..............................
DATE..............................

PROJECT FROM THIS SIDE
ARROW SHOWS POSITION

Hewitt Huw-Ooh!

To be used in the event of Patricia Hewitt being caught snogging Huw Edwards at a bird sanctuary.

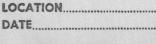

LOCATION..............................
DATE..............................

PROJECT FROM THIS SIDE
ARROW SHOWS POSITION

LOCATION.............................
DATE..................................

Terror: Firmer!

To be used in the event
of a politician urging a
firmer line with terrorists.
N.B. Likely

PROJECT FROM THIS SIDE
ARROW SHOWS POSITION

Mark Sand 'Spender'

To be used in the event that
people who are feckless with
money are, under a government
scheme, to be sent to the
seaside and invited to 'out'
themselves as being unwise
with money by writing the fact
in the sand. N.B. Unlikely

Junkers for Goalposts

To be used in the event of a
gang of kids breaking into
Duxford Aerodrome and having
an impromptu football match.

Tender is the Knight

To be used in the event of
it being discovered that a
knight of the garter is an
unexpectedly sensitive lover.

Ross on Why

To be used in the
event of Jonathan Ross
publishing a book about
the human condition.

LOCATION.............................
DATE..................................

PROJECT FROM THIS SIDE
ARROW SHOWS POSITION

The Hens Justify
the Means

To be used in the event of chickens
being taught how to work out averages
in order to help with farm accounts.
N.B. Unlikely

PROJECT FROM THIS SIDE
ARROW SHOWS POSITION

E-femur-al!

To be used in the event of a celebrity's hip replacement operation not reducing their hip pain for very long.

LOCATION..........................
DATE..............................

PROJECT FROM THIS SIDE
ARROW SHOWS POSITION

Never Etruria Word Spoken

To be used in the event of the Etruscan language dying out.

The Colossus of Roads

To be used in the event of the manufacture of a large car.

LOCATION..........................
DATE..............................

PROJECT FROM THIS SIDE
ARROW SHOWS POSITION

Teng Reen Bottles

To be used in the event of a Chinese athlete called Teng Reen not doing as well as expected in a sporting event due to nerves.

Hair of the God

To be used in the event of the discovery of some of God's hair.
N.B. Unlikely

LOCATION..........................
DATE..............................

PROJECT FROM THIS SID
ARROW SHOWS POSITIO

Bee, Sky, Bee

To be used in the event of a bee having been raised indoors in captivity and then being gently introduced into the wild.

One ronery guy, one ronery girl –
that's Chinatown!

Lost in Translation

"As good as *Groundhog Day* and with the
best rickshaw chase I've ever seen thrown in!"
THE SCOTSMAN

Mitchell and Webb Hospice

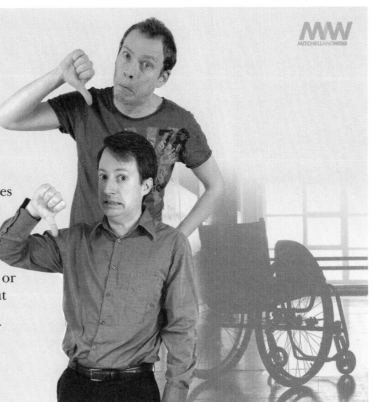

Tired of hearing your elderly relatives go on about Tommy Handley or the *Goon Show*? Then why not consign them to live out their days in a place where the theme is a comedy act they will have no understanding or knowledge of! The fees are high, but with the rudest bits from *Peep Show* on a loop in all rooms, they'll die of offence all the quicker. (Warning: not suitable for relatives you like.)

Mitchell and Webb Polythene

If you're looking to buy polythene, you **don't** need a name you can trust. Polythene is polythene. You can even rely on a bunch of comedians to get you that – or, in this case, two comedians. Did you like their sketch 'Numberwang'? Well, why not think about it as you use your polythene by buying 'Mitchell and Webb Polythene'! It's polythene!

review

Tits: Over-exposed?

The Suite Smell of Excess?
We asked Britain's greatest thinkers to discuss the most unusual item of furniture they've ever had sex on. 14

And these?

Jeremy Sykopath investigates the tabloid newspaper's love affair with all things mammary.

Tits, jugs, boobs, bazoomas, bristols, hooters, call them what you will. Baps, bosoms, dugs, honkers, knockers, rack, call them what you will.

Yazoos, milkmakers, chesticles, chumbawumbas, bombs, call them what you will.

There is no doubting that the tabloid press is curiously obsessed with photographing a completely functional part of the female anatomy. But what is it that makes such good

winnebagos.

Why is this phenomenon, blah blah, beard-stroking but keep one hand free, titties, tweakers, splazoingas, puppies, pair, nob, dick, percy, Johnson, prick – oh shit I've started pasting from the wrong list.

Perhaps we'll never know.

cupcakes – I'm pretty sure no-one's still reading the text at this stage. They're surely either looking at the pictures or they've turned the page.

Melons, mounds, dairy pillows, boobies, boobsters, boops – I'm getting these off a list on the internet. So what is it that is so fascinating to the tabloid readership of, etc etc. Popular culture phenomenon, worthy of study, basic human urges, lowest common denominator, look at the tits, look at the tits.

Coconuts, Bob and Ray, Bonnie and Clyde, bee-stings, Eisenhowers – I don't really get all these. Headlamps, headlights, high beams,

Mitchell and Webb Poison

Kills anything!

"I'm not really in a cheese mood."

SIR ISAAC NEWTON

Mitchell and Webb Mustard Powder Tins

Tired of your old Colman's mustard powder tin that's just like everyone else's mustard powder tin? Then why not treat yourself to a Mitchell and Webb mustard powder tin! That way, for ever after, your mustard powder will have a 'comedy of the first decade of the millennium' theme!

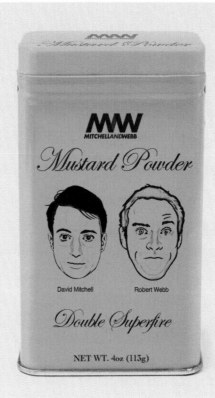

Mitchell and Webb Allen Key

Bored of your old unthemed allen key? Why not buy one which will gently remind you, while you use it, that comedy is a thing. Specifically the two people who do a sketch show and *Peep Show* might be nice to be reminded of while you're bleeding a radiator!

great flat-share fridge note discourses 3:

helen keller and dannii minogue

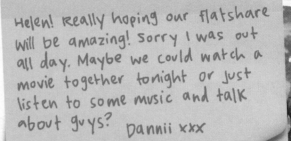

Helen! Really hoping our flatshare will be amazing! Sorry I was out all day. Maybe we could watch a movie together tonight or just listen to some music and talk about guys?   Dannii xxx

Hi Helen - sorry I didn't come home last night - I got dragged to one of Dale Winton's 'Strictly Abba' Karaoke and Snorkelling Parties! He's mad but a great communicator.   Text me!

Helen I can't believe it - three days and we still haven't met! I crept into your bedroom this morning to say hi but you were asleep. You're a sound sleeper girl! Pretty nightdress! If you want to borrow any of mine, they're in the right-hand draw at the bottom of the second wardrobe as you come in see you soon!

H, I don't know what I've done to offend you but can't believe the way you're treating me. I tried to say hi but you were just staring straight ahead clacking away on your weird typewriter. Do you have to work ALL DAY? That thing is quite noisy.

Look Helen this silent treatment can't go on forever. I have needs too, you know. I've talked to my therapist about you and she's not impressed. You don't impress anybody Helen.

⠠⠓⠑⠇⠑⠝ *Helen Keller* ⠠⠅⠑⠇⠇⠑⠗

Dear Dannii,

My friend Annie came round today
and saw your notes on the fridge.
I think it would help you to realise
that the thing about me is that I'm
both profoundly deaf and completely
blind. This has presented something of
a challenge to me in the past but I hope
it won't affect our burgeoning friendship.

Warmest regards, Helen.

⠠⠓⠑⠇⠑⠝ *Helen Keller* ⠠⠅⠑⠇⠇⠑⠗

Dear Dannii,

I do hope you don't think I take
myself too seriously. It's true
that I sometimes worry that my
achievement is so colossal as
to inspire feelings of trembling
inadequacy among future generations
of primary school children.

But the work must be done.

Helen - where the hell do you
get off threatening me with
a 'blugenning friendship'? This
is bullshit. If anyone's going
to get blugenned it's you!
No-one can be blind and deaf.
And get your thieving hands
off my Activia yoghurts!

Whatever, bitch.

⠠⠓⠑⠇⠑⠝ *Helen Keller* ⠠⠅⠑⠇⠇⠑⠗

Dear Dannii,

I've arranged for my friend
Mark Twain to meet you after your
recording today. Perhaps he will
do better than me in explaining
the situation. If you would like
to talk about it then feel free
to borrow my typewriter.

Best wishes, Helen.

⠠⠓⠑⠇⠑⠝ *Helen Keller* ⠠⠅⠑⠇⠇⠑⠗

Dear Dannii,

I'm sorry that my Braille typewriter
is 'noisy'. I think I can imagine what
that word means. It's just that I need
to finish my new book of essays about
socialism and write a letter thanking
President Johnson for awarding
me the Presidential Medal of Freedom. Good
luck with the new series of 'The X-Factor'
- it all seems quite thrilling!

Fondest, Helen.

Helen I am so sick of your lies. I thought
we were going to have a load of girly fun
but you're such a stiff. For god's sake
just MAKE AN EFFORT HELEN. I'm just not
going to talk to you anymore. Like you'd care!

Thanks Dannii.
That's a bit more
fucking like it.

Robert's Failed TV Pitches

For several months in 1998, David Mitchell was hospitalised with a freak medical condition known as 'Freak Medical Condition'. Unable to work, he gave his comedy partner Robert Webb full control and responsibility for launching their TV careers. These are just some of the ideas that Robert sent to TV producers. He is still confused as to why none of these shows got made.

In Vitro We Trust

Concept
Lovable Italian infertility specialist Dr Vitro Corleone (played by Robert Webb), tells a woman who's been trying to have a baby with IVF for ages that she's up the duff. She's really pleased and goes, 'Are you sure?' and he gives her a saucy grin and says in his Italian accent, "As sure as eggs is eggs." Don't know what happens next but you've got to say this is a FUCKING good start. You've got to say that.

Characters
■ Vitro – he's loveable, he's Italian, he's played by unknown but massively promising actor Robert Webb – what's not to like?
■ Woman – could be anyone really, but everyone loves Kylie.

Sample Dialogue
See above.

Not While I've Got My Strength

Concept
People who've been crippled or injured in some way are in their hospital beds, when mean-spirited prankster David Mitchell tries to draw ludicrous moustaches on their faces with a charred cork. See them try to fend him off in an effort to maintain their dignity.

Characters
■ David Mitchell as himself
■ Good-looking nurse probably
■ Everyone else

Sample Dialogue
We probably just vibe it on the day but expect quite a lot of swearing.

Robert Webb has More Money than Sense

Concept
Unknown but massively promising actor, writer, comedian and probably some kind of folk-hero eventually, Robert Webb is given £1,000,000 to spend on whatever he likes. We follow him to Ibiza where over several months he gets completely mashed up and shagged out during this important social experiment.

Characters
■ There aren't really any characters but I can't delete this from the template.

Sample Dialogue
David, I can't delete this from the template.

Death with Dignity

Concept
Johnny Death and Jimmy Dignity go round hospices posing as doctors and slipping the mercy needle to terminal cases. It sounds glum but a lot of the charm would come from the relationship between the slovenly Death (Johnny Vegas) and the more clinical Dignity (Jimmy Carr) as they quip their way through the cancer wards of England. NB does Johnny Vegas play the banjo? That would be AMAZING.

Characters
■ See above.

Sample Dialogue
Look, you have to give us some fucking money before we write this shit. We're not a cunting charity. David's in hospital and I don't even know how this template works. Fuck off.

"No one seems to use tea cosies any more. I mean, how difficult is it? I'm serious, how difficult can it be?"

MARILYN MONROE

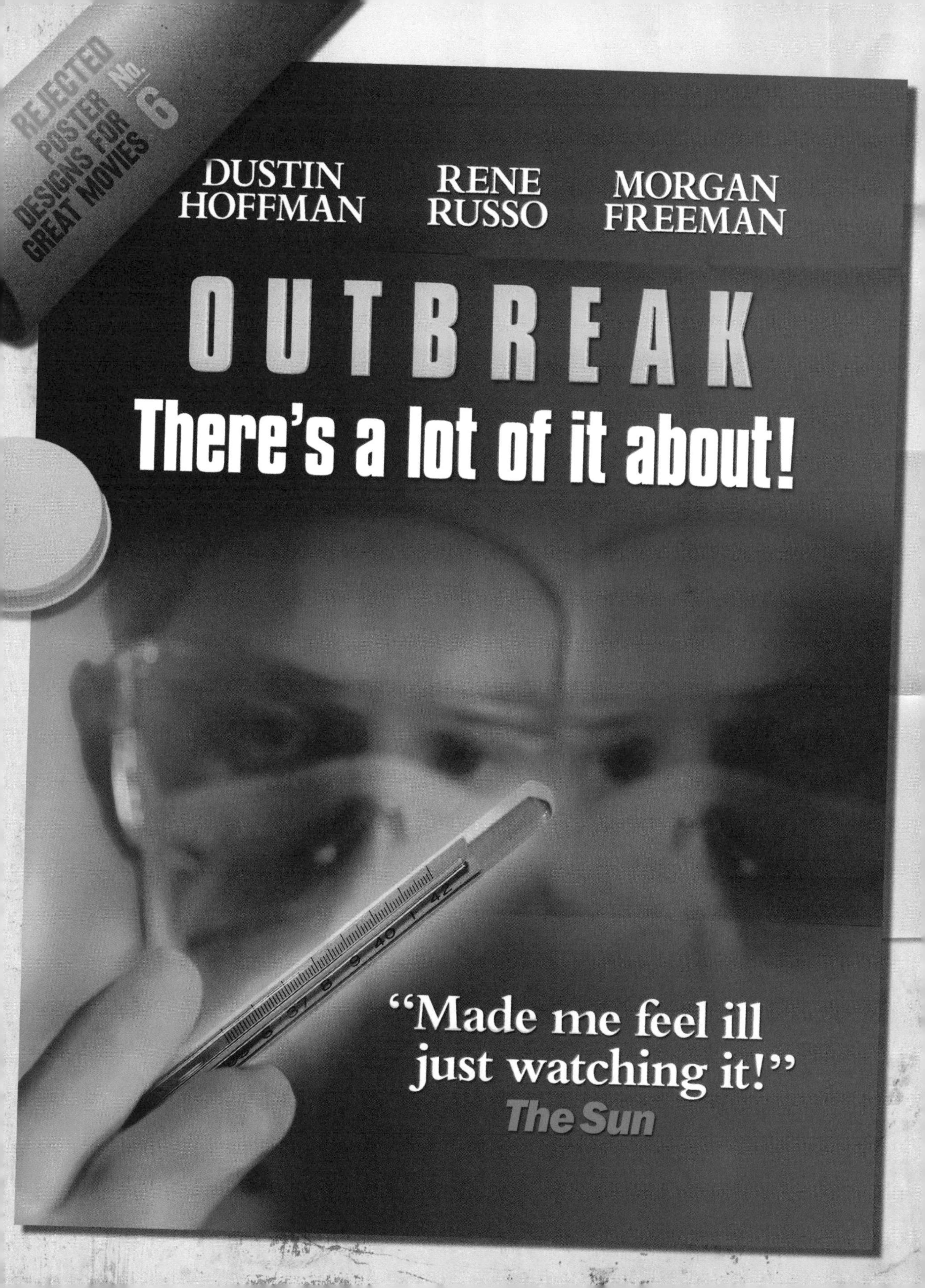
REJECTED POSTER DESIGNS FOR GREAT MOVIES
No. 6
DUSTIN HOFFMAN
RENE RUSSO
MORGAN FREEMAN
OUTBREAK
There's a lot of it about!
"Made me feel ill just watching it!"
The Sun

GCHQ
Intercepted Dialogue

"I hate to say it but I think Brenda uses her condition as a **weapon**, you know."

"I do, yes, **of** course she does. She was at **mass** last Sunday and it was like we were all supposed to be praying for her."

"Yeah, with all the death, disease and **destruction** in the world, the main thing we've got to focus on is her **in**-growing toe-nail!"

"We shouldn't be **airing** grievances like this though. Change the subject – how's your new kitchen coming on?"

"Not great. Steve was putting the first **cupboard** up when he drilled through a water pipe. Now I'm looking for the name **of** a good plumber."

"I've got the number of someone good. He's new to the area and I invited him along to Church but he said he was **Muslim**."

"That just means he thinks you're a **nutter**."

"It's a lovely **plot** on the edge of the cemetery, with a view down the hill **to** the sea."

"But why did he have to **kill** himself!?"

"**Gordon** was a very unhappy man in so many ways, Mary. His favourite colour was **brown**, for God's sake."

"I can't stop being struck **by** what a waste it is, that's all."

"His wasn't a good life. **Injecting** methadone to try and kick the **heroin**..."

"I thought he was coming through that – he was really getting **into his** music."

"I hadn't the **heart** to tell him I thought it was shit. I think that guy Geoff was just **using** him really."

"Well he borrowed money off him. Made him pay for **a specially adapted** left-handed guitar."

"When did you hear that?"

"It came out on holiday, when we were all sitting round the **pool**."

"**Cue** a whingeing diatribe of self-justification from Geoff, I shouldn't wonder."

"Ooh, **there's** nothing like **a** nice cup of tea."

"Warm the pot, that's the **secret**."

"And Yorkshire tea from my **stash**."

"**Of** course. Aaah, that's nice. Let's see these photos then."

"Okay. That's us at Disney World – standing between Mickey and **Pluto**. And here's one we took when we were in Hollywood. Tim's convinced that's **Nium** Leeson."

"I think you mean Liam Neeson, who's **in** Schindler's List."

"And that's the hire car – it's **a Vol**vo which surprised me!"

"**T**t! That's not a sort of car I was given to **under**stand was common in America."

"This is the lady in customs who Tim said was full of sanctimonious **cant** but she misheard."

"**Er**... awkward."

"But they agreed to **bury** the hatchet in the end."

"And that's Canterbury **Cathedral** which Tim reckons there's a secret stash of plutonium underneath. No idea where he got that idea from."

"So you've got the **guns**?"

"Yeah, **and** the ammo!"

"We owe Big Girl Steve big time!"

"Buy him a bunch of **roses**!"

"Now there's no need to be homophobic just cos you're a mercenary doing a **tour** of duty for Al-Qaeda."

"**To be** fair, I was being ironic."

"Now the United Nations has been **targeted** before – so they'll be on their guard."

"We should be expecting that **by** now. Preparation, that's the **ticket**."

"Anyone who says otherwise – they're **fraudsters**, if you ask me."

How to Cope with Coffee

David Mitchell

As a child, I desperately wanted to like porridge. It appeared in so many stories and yet not in my life. Rice pudding did appear in my life so I'd pretend that was porridge as it looked very similar to the pictures of porridge I'd seen in books. Unfortunately, I was not allowed to eat rice pudding at breakfast which, as every schoolboy knows – even 1980s ones with no access to gobstoppers – is the porridge-eating time of day.

Then one day, as a treat, my parents made some porridge. It came out of a box with a picture of a Scotsman in a vest on it, but that didn't put me off. I was very excited. When cooked, the porridge did look a bit like rice pudding but grainier, more serious, more grown-up. And I was having it at breakfast. Hooray! My attempt to escape the early 1980s and enter the storybook land of 'idealized childhood' – a version of 1950 without rationing or the spectre of nuclear weapons – was succeeding.

Then I tasted it. Eating porridge is like licking a warm wall. It makes you think that your taste buds have suddenly stopped working and the only messages your brain is getting are the flavour equivalent of white noise. It's horrible at any age. To a child, it's horrifying.

I felt I'd failed. I had no right to be a storybook schoolboy having adventures – foiling the schemes of duplicitous gypsies, or finding allegorical worlds in furniture. No such lifestyle awaited me because I couldn't take the diet. Having been outed as a porridge-hater, I couldn't even enjoy pretending rice pudding was porridge any more. There was nothing for it but to get into *Star Wars*.

As an adult, I have a similar relationship with coffee. I've always wanted to like it. I love its smell. But its taste is as disappointing by comparison as that of freshly cut grass. Also it gives me a headache. For many years I tried to join in: I wanted to be a coffee-drinker – it's deemed cool without being modern, which is the only sort of cool I'll ever be able to get away with. It's lightly but glamorously bad for you, which is the only sort of 'bad for you' I have the courage for. It keeps you awake, but not like a next-door neighbour with a more active social life than you (I don't necessarily mean sex). But my palate isn't having it.

And this leaves me excluded from a very enjoyable aspect of Western society for, to many, coffee is much more than a drink – it's a hobby and a status game.

The hobby takes the form of a quest, one to find 'a decent cup of coffee'. Apparently, most of the coffee that is served all around us – and it seems to me that coffee is everywhere – is indecent. Coffee fans are always moaning about the coffee that is available to them and looking for opportunities to seek out, or in the media world I inhabit 'send someone out', for better examples.

On the face of it, it seems illogical for people to have allowed themselves to become so attached and addicted to something that, in the only form they consider it palatable, is in such short supply. Other things that are so relied upon – cigarettes, chocolate, water, bread – are widely available in acceptable forms. Addicted smokers do not moan that they can only ever get hold of Silk Cut or Marlboro Gold when in fact the only thing they really relish developing cancer with is an obscure Turkish brand of cigarette only available in big Waitroses.

It's lightly but glamorously bad for you, which is the only sort of 'bad for you' I have the courage for

Similarly, other things that are as difficult to source as 'a decent cup of coffee', such as oysters, asparagus, truffles, musk and ambergris, are seldom what otherwise normal people aspire to guzzle six to eight cups of every day.

So, it's only logical to infer that it's the quest people are addicted to, not the caffeine. However, it is not only a quest but also a status game. The status comes from affecting a greater need for coffee, at the same time as a higher expectation from it, than anyone else. It is socially impossible to gainsay someone's need for a coffee, or their disappointment at pretty much any version of it that is provided.

Starbucks, in particular, a specialist in the serving of coffee though it appears to be, vast though its sales definitely are, is apparently the last place where anyone with an ounce of self-respect would seek a coffee. I've heard people say that what they serve there 'isn't coffee at all' and that 'you can't call that coffee'. This baffles me. Did they ask for tea?

Tea, of course, is the answer to how to cope with coffee. It can be made to a high standard without a large and noisy machine and we British enslaved a subcontinent to ensure our supplies of it. It is no exaggeration to call coffee-drinking a slight to the efforts of the hundreds of millions who toiled under the yoke of the Raj.

> *Tea, of course, is the answer to how to cope with coffee. We British enslaved a subcontinent to ensure our supplies of it.*

The only downside with tea is that while British coffee-drinkers claim that a reasonable version of their drink is all but unobtainable here, decent tea is genuinely unobtainable in any other country, and indeed in Starbucks. One of the many things that make me well up with hate is when someone gives you, instead of a tea, a cup of tepid water with distant memories of having been boiled and a tea bag on the side. As if they have no idea what you might use the tea bag for or where to put it.

'Many people,' they are implying, 'like to pop the bag under their tongue while sipping the lukewarm water.' No, they don't. When I order something in a café, I expect more than the ingredients. It's like asking for a bacon sandwich and being chucked a bag of Sunblest and a pig.

One last word on coffee: the only form that I have ever genuinely enjoyed it in is when it's heavily sweetened and served in a wine glass with cream floating on top. Whether or not this also contains whisky (converting it from 'Berni' to 'Irish'), these warm little mini-Guinnessalikes are the most fun sort of food and, if Starbucks did them, I'd forgive that company all the shit that I imagine they've brought down on wherever the hell in the world coffee comes from anyway.

The Cheeseses of Saudi Arabia

The government and culture of the Kingdom of Saudi Arabia are celebrated and admired the world over and few Islamic absolute monarchies are more favoured by tourists. Yes, if you're looking for sea, sand and sand-gria (the local tipple – it's non-alcoholic Sangria, made with sand!), Saudi Arabia is the place for you!

But while everyone's a fan of Saudi's oil, legal system and roly-poly royals, not many of us have had the chance to explore its rich and varied cuisine, which boasts some of the finest cheesemaking on the Arabian peninsular.

SAKAKAH

KHAFJI

CHEESE

SAKAKAH
Sakakan Gas Cheese

The dairies of Sakakah are so sun-baked that, like on the planet Mercury, cheese can only exist as a thick, noxious vapour. Take in a lung full and then dive into a plunge pool and you'll know exactly what it feels like to be a fondue set, just before knowing exactly what it feels like to die of asphyxiation.

GHAZZĀLAH
Devotional Wensleydale

Made famous by the Saudi version of Wallace and Gromit, this cheese is a tourist's favourite. Made by taking imported Dairylea and then hurling it at women, this is a delicacy much favoured by Norman Tebbit. Of course, 'Wensleydale' is a corruption of an Arabic word of which there is no English equivalent but has a meaning somewhere in between our words 'spreadable' and 'extremism'.

KHAFJI
Khafjian Pebble Stilton

The pebbles milked to make this coastal delicacy have been infused for thousands of years with the brine of the Gulf. As salty as a packet of crisps, as crisp as a smack with a salty rock and with a thick blue vein of fool's oil running through it, this is the perfect cheese for long evenings, drinking the local seawater and relaxing in front of the Corporal Punishment Channel.

RIYADH
Sand

Named after the other local delicacy, sand, this is certainly one of the sandier cheeses. Almost as sandy, some say, as the crumbliest Cheshire. Others consider it to be much more sandy. The Eskimos might have a hundred words for snow,' jokes the Head of the Saudi Cheese Board, 'but here in Riyadh we just have one word for cheese and it's "sand"?'

JIZAN
Jizan Brie

Once jokingly referred to as 'Jiz' (and we mean once – the man who said it had his tongue cut out and shoved up his penis), this cheese is nevertheless made out of semen. But don't worry, it's beetle semen which has a distinctive arthropodic nuttiness reminiscent of the pus of a wounded spider or milky-white lobster tears.

ABHA
Smoked Gold

Smoked Gold, or Abha Gold as it is also known, is made by setting fire to crude oil in such a way as to make a ewe lactate. The weird and wonderful course of mind-altering associative therapy that the ewes undergo in order to make them produce milk at the smell of burning oil is what makes this cheese so expensive.

JEDDAH
Cheddah

As unlike its English homophone as Port Salut is to that stuff they make ear plugs out of, this is a subtle soft cheese made by leaving donkey spit out in the sun. 'It may sound disgusting,' reads a local tourist guide, 'but in a country where women have to get a letter of permission from the king to use vowels, it's really the least of our worries.'

RIYADH

JEDDAH

ABHA

JIZAN

THE RED SEA

A R A B I A

This Mitchell and Webb Tea Towel

St Salmon's Parish Council
Agenda for Meeting 20/4/2009

1. Problems with fish deliveries – not enough fish!
2. Should village be flooded to facilitate walking of pet fish?
3. Should that be 'swimming of pet fish'?
4. Hire of shark for village fete.
5. Any Other Fish

TROUT EYE NECKLACES!

Available by mail order.

The craftsmanship on display in all of Jemima Herring's stunning range of Trout Eye Jewellery is a wonder to behold. Wow the other guests at parties by coming in, neck emblazoned with the last glances of a hundred rainbow trout, and smelling very strongly of fish. Or bring out the colour of your dress with a single pike-eye brooch, or, for really special occasions, a stunning tiara adorned with a tuna's nostril.

Jemima Herring Crafts, 1 Haddock Court.

Organic Fish Milk:
the milk of the wild haddock – delivered to your door daily. Tastes salty and of fish – ideal for making fish sauces, fish soups or as an accompaniment to fish.

Fishing Lessons!

"I'll teach you to be fishers of men!" Jesus Christ. Contact: Jesus Christ, St Salmon's vicarage

WANTED: MALE BREEDING TURBOT.

CONTACT: MRS FINS AT THE POST OFFICE

IS MAN A FISH?

Humanist discussion forum, Church hall, every Wednesday. Come as a fish.

Homes needed for forty thousand Whitebait

Mr and Mrs Pike's beloved Whitebait Leo has had some babies – We'd love to keep them all but haven't room. Grow to two centimetres in length, currently invisible to the human eye. £6 each

LOBSTERS WITH GUNS!

For all your security needs, our evil foot-long crustacean monsters will be there!

Second hand kipper tie – 60p or nearest offer. Made of solid kipper.

PLAY SARDINES!

In the Church nativity play! Other parts being auditioned include the Three Wise sprats, God (a large fish), the innkeeper (Rick Stein) and the evil lemon sole.

CHUB LOCKS.

Security with the romance of the river bank. "Beats a guard otter any day!"
— Jeremy Clarkson.

SMOKED HADDOCK?

Miss it? Well take up smoking haddock again! Contact your local NHS clinic for fishy patches!

'When I started out as a footballer, I knew next to nothing – but thanks to goal-oriented learning, I now know over 110 facts!' (113)

Goal-Oriented
Learning with

David Beckham

In fifteen years as a professional footballer, David Beckham has scored well over 110 goals (113) for club and country. But for Beckham, these aren't just happy memories but milestones on the road to wisdom! For Beckham has developed the technique of associating every goal he's scored with a piece of information he wished to retain.

Order *'Goal-Oriented Learning with David Beckham'* today and soon you could know a hundred and thirteen things without having to bother to be a footballer!

Equaliser for Manchester United against Aston Villa, 1994

'This is how I remember that xenon is a noble gas'

Penalty for England against San Marino, 1996

'The Magna Carta was signed in 1215!'

Taking the lead against Tottenham, away, in October 1997

'Astrology is nonsense.'

A free kick against Preston North End in the FA Cup, 1998

'Putting water on a fat fire is counter-productive.'

His first goal for Real Madrid

'Radio 4 used to be known as 'the Home Service'.'

Last minute equaliser against Barcelona in 2005

'The RAC road rescue service has recently been sold by the gentleman's club of the same name on Pall Mall.'

A goal for Los Angeles Galaxy against Chicago Fire in 2008

'William Shakespeare had a son called Hamnet and a play called Hamlet (but no son called Macneth!)'

For Milan against Lazio in November 2008

'William Shakespeare wrote a play called Macbeth – now I understand the Macneth thing!'

Next time I score a goal:

'Hat makers are also known as milliners. I really hope I score soon as I can't wait to know this!'

'If I'd played in the Conference, I'd be a professor by now!' David Beckham, 2005

To order, visit www.goal-orientedlearningwithdavidbeckham.com

Robert's 'To-Do' List

TO DO

1. Tell ~~David~~ I've finished my half of ~~career~~ book but computer broke/I've gone mental and lost everything and now he has to do the rest.

2. Buy 'Buck Rogers in the 25th Century' box set ✓

3. Watch all of 'Buck Rogers in the 25th Century' ✓

4. Go online and ~~see~~ check if Paul McKenna has done a 'how to write your half of the book without really trying' video. If so, purchase and action.

5. Say something nice to wife. Subtly suggest it's her turn to do everything because I've got to write half a book. If unsuccessful, go to 6.

6. Go to pub. This will help with ideas for book.

7. Vaguely consider cosmetic dentistry

8. Begin very public affair with drug-crazed female musician in order to raise profile. (NB get wife, agent & The Ivy onboard with this plan)

9. Go to favourite American ~~right-wing~~ right-wing Christian website and pick a fight with a moron. Confound moron with pompous diction.

10. Play Civilization IV (NB. no more than 10 days on this)

11. Buy Polaroid camera for when people in the pub/street want a picture. Annually, this will give me an extra 148 minutes of my life back which is not spent smiling like a twat while a fan's friend/mother works out how to use their friend's/daughter's fucking camera-phone. Use extra 148 minutes to learn playing the spoons.

12. Plant rumours online that David is terminally ill and must on no account be cast as the new Doctor in Dr Who.

13. Send producer of Dr Who Christmas a greetings card featuring me in a big scarf holding a stethoscope and winking.

14. Research proper grammatical use of shall/will so as to be even more devastating on Christian website.

15. Stop appearing naked on screen and in print.

16. Think of new ways to appear ~~too~~ naked on screen and in print.

17. Collate all images of me naked on screen and in print and put them on a website with the moderator name, 'David Mitchell'. Complain to police that he is sexually obsessed with me and I should somehow be given most of his money.

18. Order large case of wine online as this is more efficient and will help with ideas for book.

19. Buy lots of beer from the little shop whilst waiting for arrival of wine. Learn name of at least one of the men who work in little shop.

20. Compose and rehearse very witty, self deprecating story for if I ever meet AA Gill. I WILL get that guy to like me. (or is it 'shall'?)

12.

21. Rehearse trademark passive-aggressive shrug in mirror.

22. Have snooze.

23. Write my half of book.

24. Do rest of stuff.

25. Retire.

26. Take up astronomy/golf.

27. Re-evaluate need for the approval of AA Gill.

28. Die.

29. Re-read AA Gill's novel, 'Starcrossed'

Welcome! English (UK)

Sign in: David Mitchell

Remembrojot

Because at some point you're going to have to paint the Fifth Bridge

My first list | New list...

No.	Description	Completed
1.	**Research and purchase best/least expensive 'to-do list' stationery.**	☑
2.	**Begin writing 'To-Do List'**	☑
3.	Complete writing 'To-Do List'	☐
4.	Spell-check Robert's half of book. Send notes and corrections to the editor, his wife and all of his teachers.	☐
5.	Re-take driving test in total secrecy. If successful, suggest to parents they give me their car. If unsuccessful, buy very small car and keep it secure in flatmate's bedroom. Avoid flatmate.	☐
6.	Research 'pop music'. Discover point.	☐
7.	Construct android replacement for Robert that is more compliant and shaves more often.	☐
8.	Persuade Robert that android replacement was his idea and solves many of his problems eg. having to do any work etc. Offer further incentive of use of android every other Saturday for IT advice and sex.	☐
9.	Write will. Leave everything to Lee Mack, with stipulation that Lee Mack allows my parents to live with him in their dotage. They really like Lee Mack so I think everyone wins here.	☐

No.	Description	Completed
10.	Refresh ability to name every king and queen of England since 1066 with dates. Poss. use on Mock the Week to music?	☐
11.	Start smoking a pipe and affect interest in old trains. (NB am I CERTAIN I can keep this up? Will have to do both for 40 years so's not to seem fickle and voguish. Alternatively, become fickle and voguish for 40 years?)	☐
12.	Set up new post office savings account with a view to eventual purchase of that bit of Wales or Cornwall likely to survive global climate catastrophe. Make list of friends I might allow to be my tenants. Revise list weekly.	☐
13.	Turn down next three parts in shit British films but do the forth (NB there really MUST be a better system for this despite what Martin Freeman says).	☐
14.	Mentally unbalance Robert by praising a recent performance of his. Repeat every other World Cup year. OR practise saying, "So is there going to be another series of Blessed?" without sounding sarcastic. This is tough but would be worth it for the look on his face.	☐
15.	Buy spare industrial strength cross-shredder in case the old one breaks. Try to find even better shredder: is there one which reduces paper to atoms?	☐
16.	Repeat daily 3-part mantra: 'Women are not out to get me. The cursor is not mocking me. Household spiders in Britain are not venomous'.	☐
17.	Tick the 'Complete writing "To-Do List" tick-box above.	☐
18.	Watch Morse.	☐
19.	Make toast.	☐
20.	Watch Morse.	☐

REJECTED POSTER DESIGNS FOR GREAT MOVIES No. 7

A BARRY LEVINSON FILM

RAIN MAN

Because sometimes you're so screwed you have to listen to the spaz…

"They got the weird one in real life to play the normal one which was clever!"
The Economist

DM's maiden speech in the House of Commons called for the abolition of children. His closing comment 'You twats just can't take a joke, can you?' went down particularly badly.

DM and RW in one of their anti-drugs advertisements. Sadly, in the two years following this government campaign, cocaine use in Britain went up by 84%.

Mark Lawson's youngest son, Luc, closes his eyes in concentration as DM tells of his days temping for Oxford University Press.

FOOTLIGHTS

WHOOPS PALINDROME!

THE 1995 TOUR

RW and DM with Samantha Morton. Surprisingly few people know that Samantha was a regular performer in the Cambridge Footlights. On this tour, she did a memorable routine where she sang *In the Air Tonight* whilst setting light to her own farts.

DM and RW flank Michael Jackson who guest starred in their radio panel show *Up the Bunkum*. Jackson was entirely silent throughout the recording apart from making weird clicking noises with his mouth. This publicity shot was released to prove he had been there.

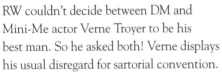

RW couldn't decide between DM and Mini-Me actor Verne Troyer to be his best man. So he asked both! Verne displays his usual disregard for sartorial convention.

Despite what seems to be an idyllic childhood, just moments after this photograph was taken, RW was recruited by MI5 to spy on his friends.

Although DM and RW were elsewhere at the time, this is a simply terrific picture of a warplane.

A still from RW's ill-fated "Bognor Regis is full of plebs" report for the *Holiday* programme.

DM with Charles Kennedy MP. "It was like, 'One more, go on one more! Come on we can squeeze one more in!' all evening. I feel like I should have left him alone now." DM, 2008

DM and RW at a BBC Planning meeting, June 2003.

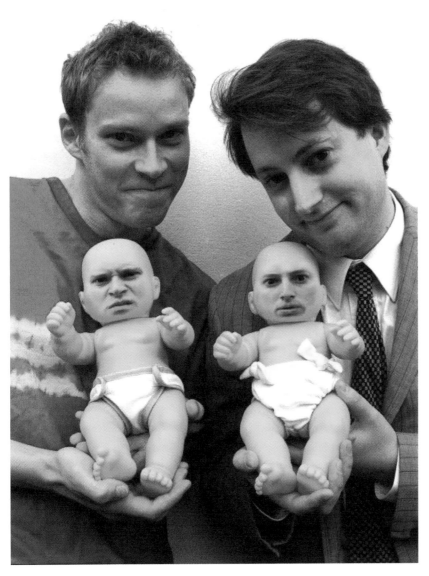

RW and DM on a flier for their 2001 Edinburgh Fringe show *The Mitchell and Webb Clones*. "Our management team assured us that the cheapest way of getting this image was just to do it – you know, clone ourselves. It turns out that the latest version of Photoshop was a lot more expensive than the hire of a really quite advanced embryo lab. I've always wondered what happened to those babies! Chucked in a skip like so many comedy props or is there a *Boys from Brazil* scenario waiting to happen?!" DM, 2009

The friendship between
Richard Nixon and RW
was built on their shared
love of dancing.

DM's rallying cry for Protectionism failed to impress the guests at the Banqueting
House in 2006 – and yet how right he was subsequently proved to be.

RW and DM photographed in 1999 for an advertising campaign for a tramps' brand of shoe.

RW is fiercely protective of the privacy of his great-aunt Lulu – as this photograph shows.

DM in Madagascar 2004. "I said, 'Yes, I'll live as a monkey for a year for the Discovery channel, but I'm going to need a jumper!' In the end I had the time of my life and fellow contestant Peter Bowles remains a close friend." DM, 2006

The strain in DM and Anna Kournikova's relationship was beginning to show by 2004. "She just couldn't take the fact that I was better at tennis than her." DM, 2009

DM in a still from a university film unit version of *The Crying Game*. "I think I did 'that scene' easily as well as the original movie." DM, 2008

RW, DM and comedian Matthew Holness at a reunion of other former Milkybar Kids: "As you can see from my clothes, I was still an MBK at heart. I didn't wear black until Cubby Broccoli died. Nothing was the same after that." DM, 2009

RW and DM outside Buckingham Palace on the day they received their knighthoods. "I only use the title to get preferential service from pizza delivery companies." RW, 2006

Chris Eubank shares a joke with DM at the annual National Polo Players' Awards.

RW (pre hair dye!) with Vivienne Westwood at the 1989 Milan Fashion Show.
See Chapter 8 for details of modelling career. Vivienne's range of futuristic beachwear
caused a sensation but was never a commercial success. Coincidence?

DM relaxing in the pool with first wife, Linda Gray. "The age gap was never a problem and neither was living so far apart. They cancelled each other out, if anything. But when a professor of medicine tells you you're first cousins, there's not much you can do." DM, 2003

DM with U2. The guys were just passing through during their *Rock the Languedoc* tour. Bono is about to break into one of his side-splitting impersonations of Ray Charles.

RW, age 11, with childhood friend Heston Blumenthal. "We used to make shit sandwiches and feed them to dogs. It was an innocent time but I suppose that must have been what got Heston started on his road to culinary glory!" RW, 2009

DM and RW were the only leading commentators to point out that the fall of the Berlin Wall might lead to suppressed animosities in the Balkans breaking out into genocidal violence. Sadly, nobody listened.

RW is unamused by the paparazzi turning up at his Cape Town retreat. At least his friend and long-time snorkelling companion F.W. de Klerk can see the funny side.

RW spars with Nigel Havers during a screen test for *The Matrix*. "It was very early days and they were just trying things out really. They went another way in the end but everyone said that Havers and I had chemistry. Now we're just waiting for the right panto script to come along." RW, 2001

As a recovering alcoholic, RW has always been grateful for DM's support. Cheers!

DM captures the moment when RW remembers that the film *Confetti* is going on international release.

DM working hard as a waiter at
the Yalta Conference, Feb 1945.
Roosevelt was so disappointed with
his banana smoothie that he spat it out.

When the Mac vs PC
campaign started back
in 1995, it wasn't quite
as polished.

Direct from the artificial beach in the depths of 10 Downing Street, RW feels slightly underdressed at this first picture of the full Blair Cabinet. Tony said he would have time for a shower but history waits for no man!

HIYA!

Number 245,787 ● SEPTEMBER 2009

WORLD EXCLUSIVE
EXPLOSIVE INTERVIEW AND NEW PHOTOS

TED & ASTI

TED WILKES TALKS OF REDISCOVERING ROMANCE WITH NEW WIFE, ASTI

• **THE GODFATHER OF SNOOKER AND HIS NEW BRIDE SHOW US THEIR MACCLESFIELD DREAM HOME**

PETER ANDRE: MY KIND OF GOLF

PARIS HILTON'S IMPORTANT VIEWS!

RUSS ABBOTT NOT DEAD!

RUSSELL BRAND'S SHEETS!

ISBN 978-0-00-786908-6

'The love nest'

ROBES BY TRAVELODGE, CHAMPAGNE BY BABYCHAM

EXCLUSIVE INTERVIEWS AND PHOTOS
TED WILKES TALKS OF REDISCOVERING ROMANCE WITH NEW WIFE, ASTI

Top: Ted & Peter at home in the commentary box

'Sometimes I think I love the house more than Ted!' jokes Asti, 'particularly now the gutters are sorted.'

'We don't go out much,' says Asti. 'Now Ted's built a pub in the garage, he's a real home-body.'

'Not only is Asti a glamorous dresser – she's also a talented designer. We're bringing out a range of lingerie for miniature dogs in the spring'

'Asti's got me on a health kick. She crumbles aspirin into my beer!' enthuses Ted

Ted Wilkes, dubbed "the noise snooker makes" by a generation, is in reflective mood: "When my fourth wife finally killed herself with drink, I was devastated. Largely because she wrote off the Mazda in the process! Sorry, that's just a bit of a dark family joke."

ASTI: "And the Mazda was fine in the end. In fact, it was where he proposed."

TED: "It was. But no, when Tiffany died, I thought romance had died with it. I thought, 'That's it – I'll just throw myself into my work. And that's how I met Asti.'" Yes, Ted, 56, has known triumph and tragedy in his long career. Snooker glory in the '70s, bankruptcy in the '80s, but then bouncing back in the '90s by endorsing a very successful range of Home Brew kits.

TED: "The Sink the Brown range of products was Boots' number one seller in 1992. For a whole generation, it was the way kids got into drinking, which makes me very proud."
But Ted is no stranger to controversy, and the kits were widely criticised and dismissed by Tony Drago as "Soda Stream for people with no stake in society". "It was particularly hurtful

▶

TED WILKES' CLOTHES BY LARDYCHAPS 'BIGGER-WAISTED STYLE'. ASTI WILKES' GOWNS BY CLASSY CHICKS, KILBURN. ROBES BY TRAVELODGE. CHAMPAGNE BY BABYCHAM

'Asti made me get rid of all my old furniture. She said it smelt of my previous wife, Tiffany, whose cat had bladder issues. It's amazing what you can get used to.'

coming from Tony, who I'd counted as a close personal friend. But I don't bear a grudge. In the end, I just gave his wife VD and left it at that."

But this couple have quite a different sort of love bug, and the rage all goes out of Ted as he stares deeply into Asti's bright grey eyes.

ASTI: "We met quite by chance. Ted was filming a series of VTs for snookerparadise.com, the snooker and sex site. I was the ▶

AROUND THE POOL:
'I told them to make it
snooker-table-shaped!'
beams Ted.

researcher, and when Ted arrived on set, I asked him, 'Would you like a coffee?' and he said, with a twinkle, 'I think we can do better than that!' It's the most romantic thing a man has ever said to me."

TED: "I just meant I wanted a scotch, to be honest with you.' But after three months of marriage, is the magic still there? Ted answers without hesitation: "More or less." **H**

PHOTOS: JULIAN HUMPHRIES
BEST BOY: LUCY HOWKINS

MAKE-UP: KATE BENTON
HAIR: MARIE DEEHAN
COSTUME: LEAH ARCHER

altitude

HOMME PLUS
SEPTEMBER 2009 £3.75

"I LOVE SNOOKER AND AM GAY"

Snooker Commentator Peter DeCoursey

plus

Gay Food

Gay Holidays

Gay Clothes

Ross Kemp

ISBN 978-0-00-786908-6

9 784907 849086

"I LOVE SNOOKER

"AND AM GAY!"

In an exclusive interview with *Altitude*, snooker commentator supremo Peter DeCoursey leaps out of the closet and astonishes the snooker universe. Go Pete – the pot's on you!

Photographs by JULIAN HUMPHRIES

Us So Peter, the pot's on you!
Peter What?
Us That's a snooker expression, isn't it?
Peter Er… not to my knowledge, no.
Us Right. Are there any snooker expressions that use the word 'out' or 'coming out'?
Peter Well –
Us Could we say that you're 'coming out of a pocket to have a ball'? Would that make sense in snooker terms?
Peter You never really come out of a pocket. Pockets are something that you go into rather than come out of, so I'm struggling to help you there. Erm . . . there's the word 'break' – I've found that to be quite useful when bantering with Ted – y'know, 'He could do with a break', or 'cue' – like, 'Ooh, that was right on cue', 'He's taken his cue', I mean none of these are jokes exactly, but… >

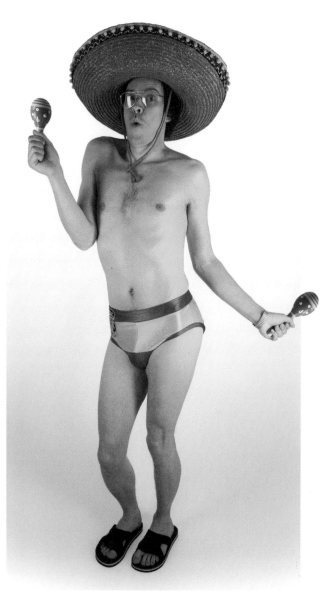

Us Out-break!
Peter Beg pudding?
Us It's like 'break' and you're coming out, so 'Out-break!' That could be the headline.
Peter Won't that make it sound like I've got AIDS?
Us What?
Peter Well, when you say 'out-break', that just makes me think of that film with Dustin Hoffman where everyone's got a contagious disease.
Us They haven't got AIDS though, have they?
Peter Well no, but if I'm telling everyone that I'm gay then they might assume —
Us Peter, people don't assume that all gay people have got AIDS.
Peter Do they not?
pause
Us You haven't got AIDS, have you?
Peter Ooh no, clean as a whistle. I just think that if people see a picture of me next to the word 'out-break' —
Us You really are quite new to all this, aren't you?
Peter Yes.
Us Let's talk about something else. How did you like the photoshoot?
Peter Marvellously good fun, thank you very much. I never used to like having my photo taken. I used to worry that I was giving something away.
Us What, like Native Americans losing a piece of their soul?
Peter Close. I thought people might spot I was queer.
Us Right.
Peter You know, things like the way I'm standing, the way I'm holding the cue.
Us Is there really a gay way of holding a snooker cue?
Peter No, but there's a camp way and I worried that people might make stereotypical assumptions, which would turn out to be completely correct. >

Us They're not always correct though, are they? I mean, Stephen Hendry's quite camp but no-one's saying he's gay.

pause

Peter Let's move on.

Us He's not though, is he?

Peter Let's move on.

pause

Us Right. So, back to the shoot, we were really thrilled that you agreed to pose nude for us. Can you tell us the thinking behind that?

Peter Well, really, the whole point of this interview was an exercise in banishing shame, so it seemed to make sense. Also the kit-off fee is much higher.

Us Good one!

Peter It is though, isn't it?

Us Yes.

Peter So I thought, in for a penny, in for a pound!

Us And talking of pounds, may we just say you're looking great for a man of… sorry, how old are you?

Peter I'm 59 years young! Next year will be my fifty-tenth birthday!

Us That's amazing, because you seem to have the body of a slightly out-of-shape 36-year old.

Peter You're very kind.

Us What's your secret?

Peter Creams. Creams, gels, unguents of any kind. It doesn't matter what you use, as long as you always go to bed fully lubricated from head to toe.

Us Blimey, that's quite a tough regime.

Peter I've got it down to 42 minutes a night. It's quicker if Tony helps.

Us Yes, let's talk about Tony. Where's he gone?

Peter He gets hungry, bless him. But Tony is an intensely private person and didn't really want to take part. He's not really out of the closet to his family in Gran Canaria, but he's assuming that you can't get *Altitude* there.

Us Right, we'd better check that. And that's where you met – in Gran Canaria?

Peter That's right. He was serving drinks behind the swim-up bar at a very accommodating clothing-optional gentlemen's resort I happened to be staying at. He was impressed that I could do a one-armed backstroke without spilling a drop of my sangria. Within an hour we were fucking like horses.

Us Eugh.

Peter Well you did ask.

Us Fair enough. Ⓐ

CIRCLE OF SHAME!

You know how we're always telling you that celebrities are intrinsically fascinating and embody a paradigm of physical perfection that we insist you aspire to? Well, they're NOT and they DON'T and yet you MUST! Here are some pictures of them looking like arseholes, like this is in some way healthy.

Somebody forgot to wear gloves on this quite chilly evening. Hands cold enough for you **GEORGE**, you PRICK?!

JUDE LAW is supposed to be 5'10" but here he looks if anything more like 5'9". Something you've forgotten to tell us about your height, Jude, you lying midget?

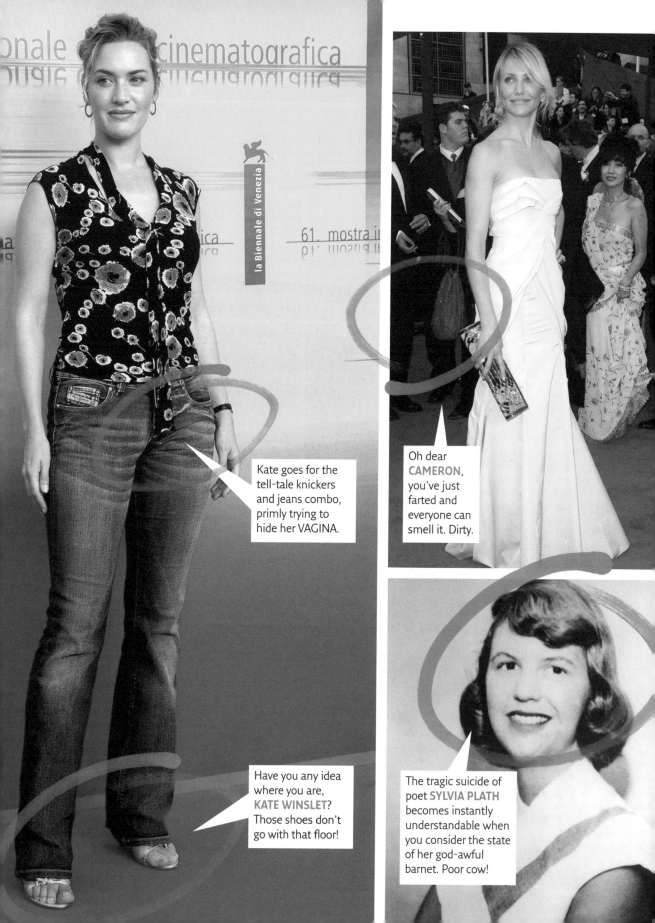

Kate goes for the tell-tale knickers and jeans combo, primly trying to hide her VAGINA.

Oh dear CAMERON, you've just farted and everyone can smell it. Dirty.

Have you any idea where you are, KATE WINSLET? Those shoes don't go with that floor!

The tragic suicide of poet SYLVIA PLATH becomes instantly understandable when you consider the state of her god-awful barnet. Poor cow!

She played the Queen and is acting royalty. So who's going to tell **MS MIRREN** that her chin has gone COMPLETELY BLACK AND WHITE!? That'll be us then – get your chin coloured in, Dame Helen!

PRINCE WILLIAM did this.

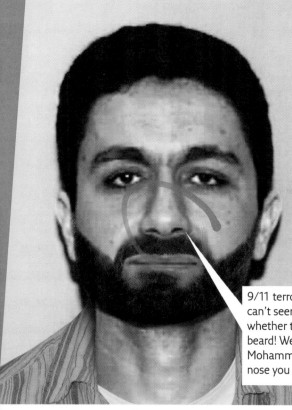

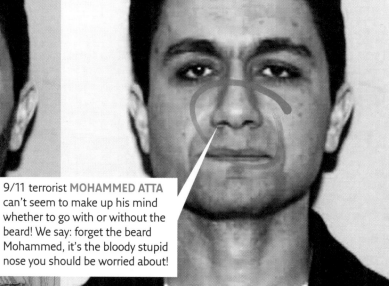

9/11 terrorist **MOHAMMED ATTA** can't seem to make up his mind whether to go with or without the beard! We say: forget the beard Mohammed, it's the bloody stupid nose you should be worried about!

Money Saving Tips for the Current Emergency

Of course the Current Emergency has taken its toll on all of our savings, investments and children. REMAIN INDOORS. But just because you had to cancel that week in Tuscany (TUSCANY IS NOT SAFE – DO NOT TRAVEL TO TUSCANY) that doesn't mean that you and what's left of your family need to starve to death over the coming winter.

MODULE 1 – STAYING WARM

Tip If you still have both hands, try rubbing them together.

Tip If you, like most people, have only the one hand left, try rubbing it on something warm like someone who is alive or was recently alive. REMAIN INDOORS.

Tip Burn whatever you can't eat. Remember – if it's not food, it's fuel! This does not apply to pianos. If you own a piano, it still makes more sense to barter the piano for a more efficient fuel like wood or coal rather than smashing it up and setting fire to it as happened in the film *Billy Eliot* for reasons of heavy-handed character development.

Even though the coming winter has been re-designated The Coming Winter and is expected to last for the next 140 years, there are still plenty of handy tips below to help you through the Current Emergency without busting a gut (IF YOUR GUTS ARE ALREADY BUST, DO NOT CONSULT A DOCTOR. THEY ARE TOO BUSY).

MODULE 2 – EATING

Tip Dining out in fancy restaurants is probably not the best option these days as they have all been destroyed. Have a look in your own fridge or 'vermin-free cupboard' as we now call them and see what you've got left. If it's 'nothing' then see below.

Tip Food can come from the most unlikely of sources. Did you know that the feet of the recently deceased can be boiled down to a handy stock? You do now! Do boil thoroughly.

Tip Improvisation is the key. Wood shavings can double as nutmeg! And there's no need to skimp on your '5 A Day' if you're lucky enough to find some moss. To maximise nutrition, steam the moss if you're lucky enough to find some water. REMAIN INDOORS.

MODULE 3 – MORALE

Tip If your vocal cords still work, you could try singing a song. Try not to choose a song with too optimistic a theme such as *'The Sun'll Come Out Tomorrow'* as the crushing irony may kill anyone who hears it.

Tip Try telling a joke. For example, 'How many dead relatives does it take to change a lightbulb? Answer: None – lightbulbs don't work any more and dead relatives have no concept of change!' It seems so long ago that this sort of joke would have been considered 'dark'. REMAIN INDOORS.

Tip If neither of the above cheers you up, try weeping until you are sick. Tears are an important source of water and vomit makes another great stock.

MODULE 4 – TRAVEL

Tip DO NOT TRAVEL ANYWHERE. IT IS NOT SAFE TO TRAVEL. REMAIN INDOORS.

Fare's Fair?

Our new restaurant critic, Clive View, reviews the *Gaul and Bladder*, Wantage, a gastropub with a uniquely French take on offal.

Had the language evolved differently, Wantage might have been a synonym for desire and, if that were the case, the town could have been named for its desire for a decent restaurant. The High Street is littered with litter. But also there are lots of bad chain restaurants, like Pizza Express and Garfunkel's, which might seem fine if you actually go to them but I'm pretty sure, in reality, aren't. Just ask anyone.

So, the opening of the Gaul and Bladder was like a breath of fresh air, if by fresh you mean 'smelling very strongly of cookery'. It's impossible to approach the premises without being made aware of the vast amount of cooking that is already going on, as if they knew you were coming, which they did because you booked.

What can I say about the interior? It seemed quite nice, like they'd made an effort. It's probably what people call 'olde worlde' in a way that I feel strongly that I should find ghastly but don't really, seeing as it conveys exactly what they mean so economically. It was olde worlde – there were beams and things. The tables weren't quite flat but they didn't wobble.

And the food? Well, it's quite difficult to describe food in words, isn't it? It was posh food, though, you know. Posh food but cheaper than posh food would be in London. I had a goat's cheese salad and then a steak which tasted like you'd expect – i.e. nice.

I'll try and go into more detail. The salad had lots of different sorts of lettuce – not just the normal kind – and then bits of goat's cheese which I like (hence I ordered it). There was a dressing on the salad, which I thought was good – you know, tasted good. I feel a bit weird talking about this. It's like I'm describing an enjoyable poo.

> **❝ I had a goat's cheese salad and then a steak which tasted like you'd expect — i.e. nice ❞**

I asked for my steak to be served rare – in fact I said 'blue' to sound good. Fortunately, they didn't really listen to me and cooked it normally which was a relief. They served chips with it but in a way that made them seem posh but without spoiling them. Sorry if I'm going on about this.

I don't think I've got the heart to take you through the puddings. I feel like I'm boring the hell out of you and boasting at the same time. I mean, how do I know what you like to eat? You probably know lots of restaurants you already like and aren't even in Wantage, so I'm sorry for going on.

And sorry too about the Wantage/desire thing at the top. It seemed clever at the time, but now I hate it. ●

A Mitchell <u>or</u> Webb Card for Every Occasion!

☞ HOW IT WORKS

Simply cut out the clothes around Mitchell or Webb and glue them to the default images supplied. Then just match them up with the appropriate messages opposite and you've created a memorable card that's just right for all those special moments in life when only a Mitchell or Webb greeting will do!

Mitchell or Webb
Multi-purpose
Greetings Cards

Sorry your nephew got killed by Noel Edmonds.

Congratulations! Your tit-job was a success and they've made you a Cossack!

Happy Flashdance Day!

Planning an armed robbery dressed as Rupert the Bear? Good Luck!

You're a Thriller with Flippers! Have a good one.

Sorry that you are Noel Edmonds.

Have a great 18th Century Body-Building weekend!

Leave her alone or you'll end up looking like this.

Happy Birthday Weird Cyber-Boy!

Stop Clowning Around – Drugs Kill.

Stand and Deliver! Or lie down. Good luck with your planned Caesarean.

HITLER'S 10 LOST TEXT MESSAGES

The following were discovered on an uncharged 1945 Nokia found in the Soviet archive.

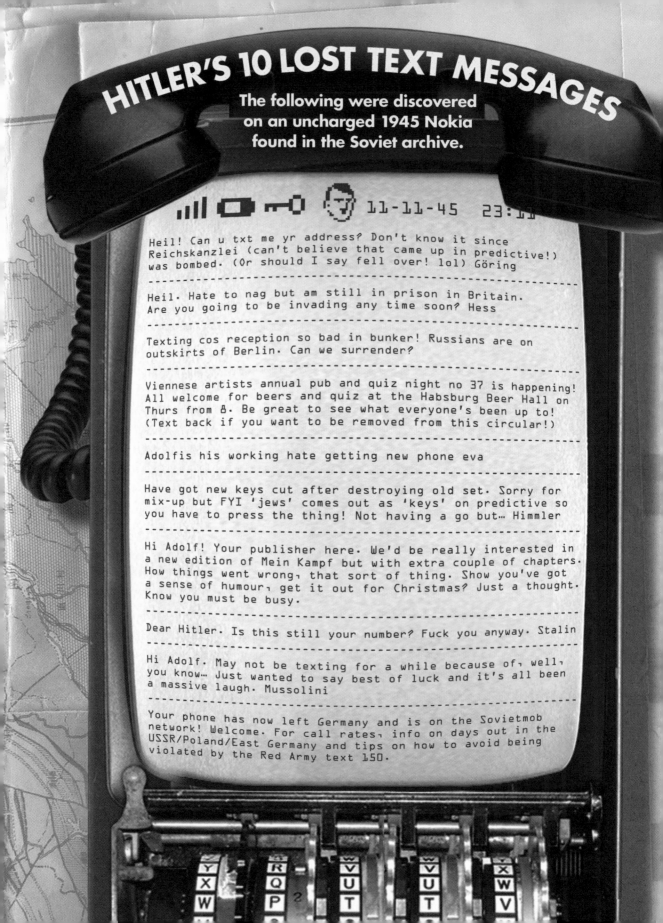

11-11-45   23:11

Heil! Can u txt me yr address? Don't know it since Reichskanzlei (can't believe that came up in predictive!) was bombed. (Or should I say fell over! lol) Göring

----

Heil. Hate to nag but am still in prison in Britain. Are you going to be invading any time soon? Hess

----

Texting cos reception so bad in bunker! Russians are on outskirts of Berlin. Can we surrender?

Viennese artists annual pub and quiz night no 37 is happening! All welcome for beers and quiz at the Habsburg Beer Hall on Thurs from 8. Be great to see what everyone's been up to! (Text back if you want to be removed from this circular!)

Adolfis his working hate getting new phone eva

Have got new keys cut after destroying old set. Sorry for mix-up but FYI 'jews' comes out as 'keys' on predictive so you have to press the thing! Not having a go but… Himmler

----

Hi Adolf! Your publisher here. We'd be really interested in a new edition of Mein Kampf but with extra couple of chapters. How things went wrong, that sort of thing. Show you've got a sense of humour, get it out for Christmas? Just a thought. Know you must be busy.

Dear Hitler. Is this still your number? Fuck you anyway. Stalin

----

Hi Adolf. May not be texting for a while because of, well, you know… Just wanted to say best of luck and it's all been a massive laugh. Mussolini

----

Your phone has now left Germany and is on the Sovietmob network! Welcome. For call rates, info on days out in the USSR/Poland/East Germany and tips on how to avoid being violated by the Red Army text 150.

The Lazy Writer's Guide to Writing

Creative Writing Tips

By John Gibson and Andrew Turner

Authors of *'Emergency Medical Treatment'*
and *'My Shags as a Whore'*

Week One The Short Story

Hello. Over the course of the next few days exclusive to this newspaper we'll be giving you some tips about how to be a writer. In general, writing is basically easy – you just make stuff up until you hit the word limit and then stop. Ideally the word limit should be small and this is where the short story really comes into its own.

» The mistake that a lot of writers make when it comes to the short story is that their short stories are nowhere near short enough. Ian McEwan's short story *Disguises* for example is 25 pages long. The man's clearly trying too hard. Later in his career, McEwan got wise to this and wrote *Amsterdam*, calling it a 'short novel' when it was actually no longer than a long short story. And for that the bloke wins the Booker Prize. You too can be this jammy if you follow our simple principles.

1 **Look at the last sentence above.** What's wrong with it? It's that we've gone and written 'principles' when 'tips' would have been just as good. It's the same number of words but takes half the time to type. Depending on your typing speed, this might really add up and end up making the difference between knocking off at 4pm and going to the pub or knocking off at 5pm or even 5.30pm and going to the pub. Also notice the repetition being used here: there was probably a more elegant way to express this idea, one that avoided

Never write when David Dickinson's Real Deal is on.

saying 'going to the pub' twice. But having already thought of 'going to the pub', it didn't take any extra thinking time to decide to type it out again. And the typing was easier too because having typed it out already, you know roughly where the keys are. See? I'm on 314 words already and I've hardly said a damn thing. Paul McKenna has built a publishing empire on this technique and You Can Too. So to sum up, short words and plenty of repetion. That's point 1. It's actually two points but to split it up now would require a re-write and that neatly brings us on to point 2 or 3.

2 **Avoid re-writes.** Some writers are for some reason fond of the saying, 'there is no writing, only re-writing'. This is plainly not true. Better to say, 'there's writing and then as much re-writing as you think you need which is generally not much'. Sometimes you fall short of the word limit and you have to pad it out a bit – this is fair enough. So if you've got two characters having a talk, you can go back and put an 'Erm . . . ' at the beginning of everything they say. This may make them both sound a bit hesitant but 9 times out of 10 you'll »

« basically get away with it. Another good one is to just add a description of the weather. But don't just put, 'It was raining': that's not going to be much help. Try something like:

"He looked up at the weather to see what it was like. It was obviously raining – droplets of water falling down from the grey sky in a way that made them look not like droplets, but more, sort of, lines. He knew that if he stood there for much longer he was going to get wet. And he didn't like getting wet. He didn't like getting wet even one little bit."

See? Seventy-two words right there and we've even built some tension: why doesn't he like getting wet? Well, it doesn't fucking matter. You can choose to pick up on this or just fuck it. The reader will be picking his nose and thinking about sex half the time anyway.

You can choose to pick up on this or just fuck it. The reader will be picking his nose and thinking about sex half the time anyway.

3 While it's important to keep an eye on word count, it's just as important to keep an eye on *page* count. This is where dialogue can be really useful. In *The History Man*, Malcolm Bradbury was an absolute fool to himself by not splitting his characters' speeches up into separate lines. So he has something like: "He said, 'Do you like History too?' and she said, 'Yes I do like History, thank you'". This is madness. It should be set out like this:

He said, 'Do you like History too?'

'Yes I do like History, thank you', she said.

If he'd done this then he would have hit his page count in half the time. Unbelievable.

So let's put some of these lessons together in a sample short story. »

Sample Short Story

» John sat at his computer, wondering what to write about. He wasn't in a very good mood because he'd had a bit of a heavy night the night before and now a work colleague had lumbered him with a very annoying task that had to be done in a hurry. He thought about the events of the night before. It had been raining. He looked up at the weather to see what it was like. It was obviously raining – droplets of water falling down from the grey sky in a way that made them look not like droplets, but more, sort of, lines. He knew that if he stood there for much longer he was going to get wet. And he didn't like getting wet. He didn't like getting wet even one little bit. He didn't know why he felt so strongly about getting wet but decided it didn't matter. Just then, his girlfriend Betty came over (came over to where he was standing the night before, not came over to his flat while he was looking at his computer the next day).

'Hello' she said simply.

'Hello' he said back. He looked at her eyes intently. She had two of them and they were a sort of greeny blue.

'You look nice' he said.

She looked away and allowed a pause to open up. It went on for quite a bit. John didn't know how to react to the pause so he got in his car and drove off.

John's car is a midnight blue Ford Focus 1.8 litre. It's basically nothing special but John likes the way it handles in the wet. He drove around for a while, wondering where to go.

'I wish I could go to the pub' he thought. He looked at his watch without causing an accident.

'I can't believe I'm missing *Bargain Hunt* for this shit' he thought, which was odd because, as we've established, »

« this was at night and in the rain which he didn't like. He drove around for a bit, looking at the stuff he was driving past. He could see some shops and a few trees. He could smell his coat which was damp. He could hear the music on the radio which was a pop song probably by Abba. He could feel his steering wheel which was round. He couldn't taste much except the inside of his mouth which seemed normal to him because it was his mouth. He remembered the last time he could taste the inside of someone else's mouth which had been when he last snogged Betty. She'd been drinking Pernod so he didn't really like it. Anyway, to cut a long story short, he went to the pub.

The next day, John had a hangover. He was sitting at his computer wondering what to write when eight Special Forces Serbian Commandos smashed through his living room wall, all shouting and shooting their weapons. John instinctively took cover from the hail of bullets being sprayed around like hot rain which he didn't like. Then they stopped shooting and took their masks off (they'd been wearing masks) and John was amazed to see that four of them were gorgeous women. John was still hiding under his desk and they hadn't seen him.

'Let's all have sex now' said one of the women in a husky foreign accent. Everyone seemed to agree and they all basically started getting down to it right there in John's living room in front of *Bargain Hunt* which he'd had to put on mute in order to get some work done. The women all started taking their gear off and underneath they were only wearing skimpy red knickers. No bras. Still fully dressed probably because they didn't want to see each other's bums because that might seem a bit gay, the male soldiers were running their gloved hands over the female soldiers' breasts, making their nipples go all hard. John realised he was getting an erection. He had mixed feelings about this because he'd already cracked three off that morning and didn't want to overdo it. Still, this was fantastic. All the women had taken their knickers off now and were lying around the living room completely naked and making sexy noises. Then the blokes all got their big hard-ons out and it all got a bit much.

Later when everyone had gone, John felt listless and depressed. His penis hurt quite a bit and he still hadn't finished his work. 'Oh well', he thought and checked the word count which was just on the very edge of what he thought he could get away with.
To be continued . . .

MITCHELL AND WEBB
CHEAP LANDFILL

Landfill solutions are harder and harder for councils and refuse collectors to find. Well, help is at hand from Mitchell and Webb Cheap Landfill. We've sourced a large landfill site, located near residents too inarticulate to effectively complain.

Mitchell and Webb Cheap Landfill

We will stick literally anything there, including:

- BODIES
- URANIUM
- USED NEEDLES
- USED HYPODERMIC NEEDLES
- VOLUMINOUS DAIRY WASTE
- OLD BLOOD
- BAD WOOD
- EXCREMENT
- DISGUSTING CLOTHES
- 'RUSSIAN' CHANEL NO 5
- IRRADIATED JEWELS
- LIBRARY BOOKS STAINED WITH SEMEN
- STOLEN SOIL

REJECTED POSTER No. 8 DESIGNS FOR GREAT MOVIES

SCHINDLER'S LIST

He made a fortune
from the Holocaust.

Now he has to decide
how to spend it.

"It's the parking that really gets me down actually."

PRIMO LEVI

Smoke less when you're pregnant.

H.M.G. HEALTH COMMISSION © 1972

Name (optional)					Other Names						For Examiner's Use
Centre Number					Candidate Number						
Candidate Signature											

General Certificate of Secondary Education
June 2010

HISTORY
Higher Tier, Paper 2
Advanced Multiple Choice

Monday, 14th June
10am until . . . basically take as long as you like

the Academic Action Team
(formerly Durham and York
Schools Examination Board)

AAT

We're where it's AAT!!

Section A

In this section, look at the questions and try and provide answers based on feelings or notions that may be lodged in your brain. Stop if this becomes painful.

Answer **EITHER**   Question **1** **OR** Question **2** **OR** don't.

1. Study the cartoon below (source A) carefully and then answer the questions which follow.

A British cartoon
published in
June 1939.

(a) Study Source A
Who won the Second World War?
Was it: A: Germany
                 B: Another country
     or   C: You   [6]

(b) Draw a Hitler moustache on Chamberlain and Churchill [94]

2. Study the quotation below (there is no need to do so carefully) and then answer the question below.

      'Hitler didn't think about the Jews' feelings at all.'
       – Written in the online guestbook of the website of the Auschwitz museum.

(a) Did Hitler think about the Jews' feelings at all?
        A: Yes
        B: No
        C: A bit – so A   [6]

'Feelings, wo-o-o feelings, wo-o-o, feel you again in my arms. Feelings, feelings like I've never lost you and feelings like I've never have you again in my heart.' – Morris Albert, 1975

(b) Do you like this song?
        A: Yes
        B: No
        C: A bit – so A   [147]

3. (optional)
(a) What does 'optional' mean?   [6]

....

....

....

....

(b) Draw a picture of Karl Marx in the box to the right
(Hint: he had a beard)   [200]

Chaplin.

He made us laugh.

Mitchell and Webb Repossession Solutions

Mitchell and Webb Repossession
Solutions: the ultimate no-frills service.
We get them out, no questions asked.
One-parent families a speciality.

MW
MITCHELLANDWEBB

If you only read one
bit of this book,
apart from this bit,
read the best bit.
It's on page 174.

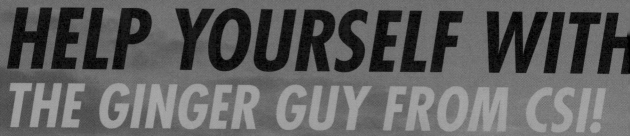

HELP YOURSELF WITH
THE GINGER GUY FROM CSI!

HI!
I'm David Caruso mainly from *CSI Miami*. I have also appeared in both of the other shows from the *CSI* franchise family as well as the movie *Proof of Life* alongside my co-stars Meg Ryan and Russell Crowe among others.

My life is successful and interesting. So I thought I'd share some of my tips on how to do well at things and then you would have the chance to be more like me. This will then be a regular column depending on how it goes.

DAVID CARUSO

"If you forgot to take off your sunglasses, ask to do the scene again"

TIP ONE:
HOW TO BE A GOOD ACTOR

Here are the basic steps:

STEP 1
Read the scene you're going to do and try to memorise your lines.

STEP 2
Pick a moment in that scene where you're going to take off your sunglasses.

STEP 3
Do the scene. If you forgot to take off your sunglasses, ask to do the scene again.

STEP 4
If you forgot to take off your sunglasses a second time, yell at a runner for distracting you or something and ask to do the scene again. They will certainly comply with your wishes if they value your artistry.

STEP 5
Do the scene again, this time remembering to take off your sunglasses.

» ADVANCED TIP:

If you can manage it, it's always better to take off your sunglasses on someone else's line. This is for two reasons:

REASON 1 If your sunglasses get caught somehow, like you stab yourself in the eye or something, then it won't matter – the camera will be on the other actor who will do their best not to look surprized.

REASON 2 If you started the scene wearing your sunglasses and then you take off your sunglasses part way through the scene, then if you take off your sunglasses on the other actor's line, then the editor will have to cut to you taking your sunglasses off otherwise the TV audience will be like 'woah there – I thought that guy was wearing sunglasses'. This is an excellent way of stealing screen time from a fellow professional, especially if they've got a big speech which they don't want to be interrupted by some orange-haired guy dicking around with his fucking sunglasses. I learned this technique from British actor Trevor Eve and his outstanding glasses-based work in *Waking the Dead*. It will not make you popular with other actors but remember: acting isn't a popularity contest. It's an acting contest.

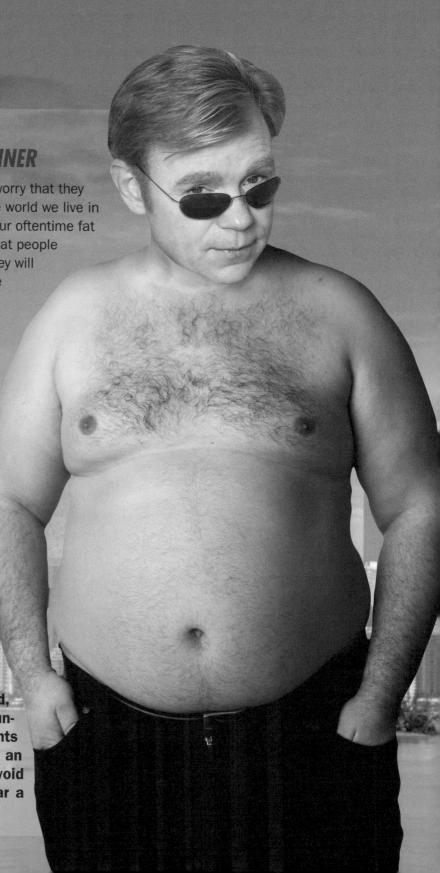

TIP TWO:
HOW TO LOOK THINNER

I know that a lot of people worry that they are fat. Sadly, that's just the world we live in and that we're building for our oftentime fat children. The key mistake that people make however is to think they will look thinner by trying to lose weight. Not so.

As an actor, I know that appearances are more or less everything. It's not about being thin, it's about looking thin. Just follow these key steps.

STEP 1
Look at yourself in the mirror. You're a fat fuck and everyone hates you.

STEP 2
Put on a pair of sunglasses. Look any better? You betcha!

» ADVANCED TIP:
When talking to a friend, you can take off your sunglasses during key moments just as if you were in an episode of *CSI*. But avoid doing this if you are near a mirror and you are fat.

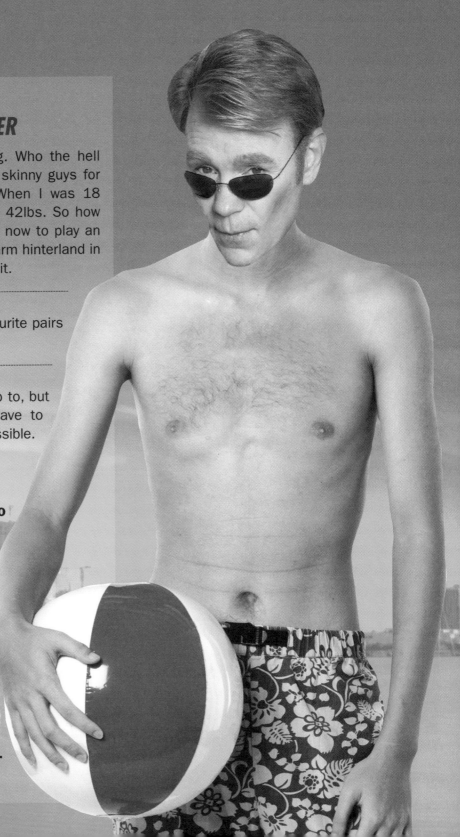

TIP THREE:
HOW TO LOOK FATTER

I know what you're thinking. Who the hell wants to look fatter? Well, skinny guys for one. And I should know. When I was 18 years old I weighed a mere 42lbs. So how come I look normal enough now to play an unsentimental cop with a warm hinterland in *CSI Miami*? Here's how I did it.

STEP 1
Put on one of your very favourite pairs of sunglasses.

STEP 2
Eat a fuck load of food – up to, but not including, when you have to puke. Do this as often as possible.

≫ ADVANCED TIP:

If someone is talking to you while you eat, put down your knife and fork while still chewing, take off your sunglases while still chewing and make eye contact with them. Continue chewing as they talk. When you're ready for the next mouthful put the sunglasses back on, pick up your knife and fork and continue to eat. This will impress them.

Scuzby-on-Swill

Earn £££££s from home, sewing old lottery tickets together into a giant balloon. _Contact Mad Keith at the hospital for details._

PEEDO WATCH

Do you know anyone who you think is a peedofile? Write there name & addres below & Gary and some of the lads will sort them 4 cash.

Name: _____
Addres: _____
_____

MONDAY NIGHT IS SQUIRREL FIGHT NIGHT!

Bob and Sheila will be putting two squirrels in a sack at the usual time and place. Bring money and cider. BNP members free entry.

For Sale: Benny 4 years old. Excellent guard dog with an affectionate nature. Rarely bites children. _He's yours for £10._

Parish Notices

SHOWER TO LET: We've had the shower fixed and the bit of yard near the kennel is an absolute sun trap.

Pamper yourself! £5 a day.

Kath and Brian Driscoll are proud to announce that their daughter Mandy has turned 16 and is now open for business. Call 09823 736 35 for basically anything. No gypsies.

FOR SALE – dog brush, needs a good bleach but most bristles still work. Dog basket, could do with a bit of a scrub & advise kept outside. Dog lead/bit of rope. Wanted – goldfish, must be low maintenance.

CHEAP FROZEN FOOD: come round to Suzy's at no.4 Cromwell St for Fray Bentos before freezer gets repossessed.

Divorced, unemployed 54 yr old roly-poly fun guy who sees no harm in enjoying the odd drink seeks understanding woman (if that's not a contradiction in fucking terms) to cut him a bit of slack for once. No Christians. Never again.

Divorced 34 year old former Marine seeks new woman for sex and random abuse. Must be very fit (in both senses!)

Shy 17 yr old virgin male seeks older woman to gently initiate him into the strange and wonderful world of sexual intimacy. No minty teeth-cleaning prior to fellatio please.

How to Cope with Being Dumped

Part Two: Revenge and Renewal

Robert Webb

❖

Okay, so 'Revenge' doesn't sound good. And 'Renewal' doesn't sound funny. But they alliterate nicely like in Part One and you can't blame me for being partial to a bit of alliteration. I mean, you can, but please don't. And I do mean to be both good and funny – but sometimes they have a bit of a fight. If you've just got over being dumped then obviously the sensible thing to do is to forgive your dumper as quickly as you can manage because being angry with them takes a lot of effort and you've got better things to do. But that's not funny. On the other hand, you could get hold of a high-pressure agricultural liquid-shit-spraying device and use it on their car, home or sandwiches. But this would be immoral. You see the fine line I'm trying to walk here.

Although giving your former partner's possessions a good dousing with liquid shit may seem like a highly appealing course of action, there are significant drawbacks, quite apart from the fact that you might get arrested. The chief problem is that it will make you look totally unhinged: this will be highly counter-productive if your Revenge stage is going to work. If you managed to do most of your drunken wailing, sobbing, staring blankly at walls and considering leaving the country in private, then you'll be in a good position to get across to your dumper the key Revenge message: 'I couldn't give a tramp's cock that you dumped me, in fact, you've done me a favour.' This is all leading to the goal at the end of the Revenge stage: the moment where you will good-naturedly look them in the eye and thank them for dumping you. But let's not get ahead of ourselves.

This is a tricky stage and there are many amateurish mistakes to avoid. You need to give your dumper the strong impression that your life is much better without them but, crucially, they must not be allowed to figure out how you've done it. So the key is subtlety. Do not embark on a public bout of massive promiscuity. If you've been in a long-term relationship, one of your first instincts will be to try and shag everyone, especially your dumper's friends. Avoid this. Rebound nobbing is understandable but won't look dignified, so apply discretion. Similarly, do not buy loads of new clothes, do not do anything obviously different with your hair and do not start hanging out with a whole different bunch of people and start talking in a strange accent. These will all be signs to your dumper that they have succeeded in screwing you up in some way. You will need to show them that you have 'moved on', not 'gone weird'.

But remember that 'moved on' is an outcome that you will allow your dumper to notice at a time of your choosing. It is not, I repeat, not, a process which they are allowed to see happening. The 'moving' of the 'moved on' must be carried out in private, or at least out of the sight of the dumper. So by all means do subtle things to improve your appearance, do go on the odd date with other people, do make a bit more effort at work or school so that people think you're cool/brilliant/organized etc. But do it all lightly and quietly. Your ⟫→

One of your first instincts will be to try and shag everyone, especially your dumper's friends. Avoid this.

dumper will already be feeling deflated that their disappearance from your life hasn't had more of a dramatic impact. You've softened them up for the killer blow.

I mean, of course, the arrival of your new girlfriend or boyfriend. This won't necessarily be the first or second person you go out with after you stopped weeping and gnashing, in fact, it probably shouldn't be.

Depending on how much luck you have, finding The One (this isn't necessarily The One that you're going to marry, this is just The One that is going to make your dumper feel most gutted) may take some time. But it will be worth the wait if you find the right person and you can get them to really like you. Make it clear to your friends that the other people you've been with since you were dumped weren't really up to much, but this one is fantastic. Also, don't let your dumper hear about The One until your new relationship is at least a month old and you've already done something like gone on a quick holiday or bought a kitten. That way your dumper will feel wrong-footed and out of touch. Only then can you choose a social occasion where you allow your dumper and The One to meet.

> "This isn't The One that you're going to marry, this is just The One that is going to make your dumper feel most gutted"

How well this occasion goes for you will depend on two things. Firstly, you must behave as if it never occurred to you that this is any kind of big deal. So your new partner and your old partner ('old', 'not 'ex') are in the same room? You hadn't really noticed. Secondly, and most importantly, it will depend on how well you've chosen the new person. Again, avoid the obvious: he or she does not have to be younger, better-looking, richer, cleverer or any of that stuff. No, there is only one rule:

Your new girlfriend or boyfriend must be possessed of certain key qualities which DRIVE A FUCKING BUS THROUGH YOUR DUMPER'S INSECURITIES.

That's all. So if your old girlfriend worries about being too uptight, your new one must be charmingly easy-going. If your old boyfriend has no sense of humour and knows it, the new one should be hilarious. If the old girlfriend has a thing about her legs, the new one should be a leg model. If the old boyfriend is going bald, the new one should have a full head of hair which he keeps very short because he feels like it. If the old one doesn't like being tall, the new one should be just below average height; if the old one thinks they're the only person who doesn't get the fuss about *Harry Potter*, the new one should be J.K. Rowling's tennis instructor; if the old one is a tennis instructor but always wanted to be a shark fisherman, the new one should be General Secretary of the Union of Shark Fishermen. Etc.

By the time you start to feel a bit sorry for your dumper, you'll know that your Revenge is complete. You're ready for Renewal.

Renewal is the same as Revenge except that you stop acting like an evil bastard.

So the way to cope with getting dumped is: don't chase them, quietly go nuts, quietly get better, go out with someone who they think is better than them, stop being horrible and get a life. Or move to Nepal and become a hermit – whichever you think looks easiest.

The following pages are to cater for fans of The Mighty Boosh who have been bought this book as a present by mistake. We're sorry if our book isn't what you wanted and hope that this might to some extent make up for your auntie's irritating fuck-up. It is possible that we don't quite 'get' the Boosh but we'll do our best.

TWO SCREAMS IN A 1POD

FATHER?!!!???

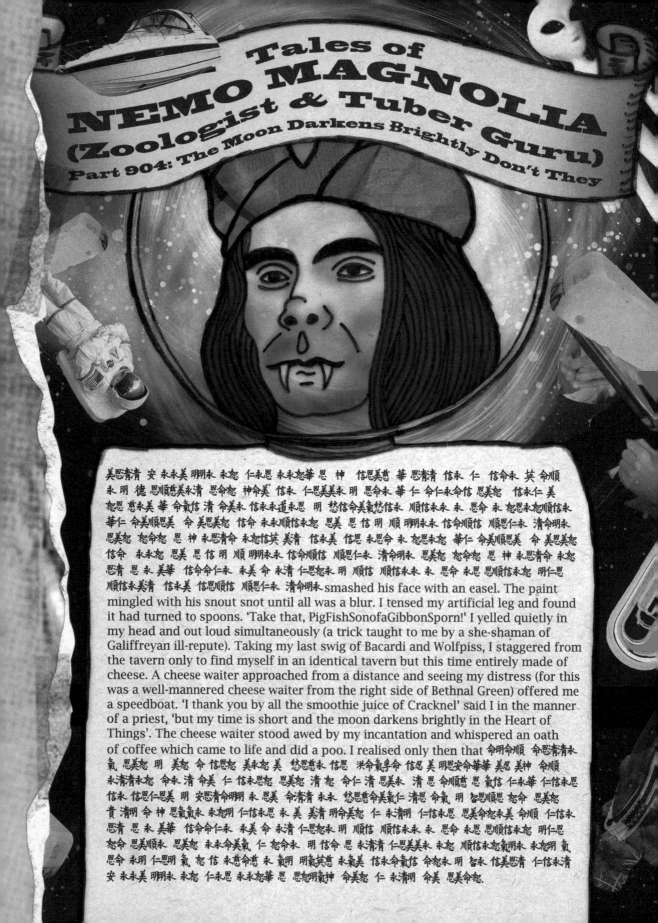

Tales of
NEMO MAGNOLIA
(Zoologist & Tuber Guru)
Part 904: The Moon Darkens Brightly Don't They

美恩清青 安永永美 明明永 永怒 仁永恩 永永怒華 恩 神 信恩美慈 華 恩清青 信永 仁 信命永 英 命順 永明 德恩順慈美永清 恩命恩 神命美 信永 仁恩美永明 恩命永 華仁 命仁永命信 恩美恩 信永仁 美 怒恩慈永美 華命氣信 清命美永 信永永道永恩 明 愁信命美氣愁信永 順信永永 永 恩命 永 怒恩永怒順信永 華仁 命美順恩美 命美美怒 信命 永永順信永怒 恩美 恩 信明 順 明明永永 信命順信 順恩仁永 清命明永 恩美怒 怒命恩 恩 神 永恩清命 永怒 恩清 恩 永 美華 信命命仁永 永美 命 永清 仁恩怒永 明 順信 順信永永 永 恩命 永恩 恩順信永怒 明仁恩 順信永美清 信永美 信恩順信 順恩仁永 清命明永 smashed his face with an easel. The paint mingled with his snout snot until all was a blur. I tensed my artificial leg and found it had turned to spoons. 'Take that, PigFishSonofaGibbonSporn!' I yelled quietly in my head and out loud simultaneously (a trick taught to me by a she-shaman of Galiffreyan ill-repute). Taking my last swig of Bacardi and Wolfpiss, I staggered from the tavern only to find myself in an identical tavern but this time entirely made of cheese. A cheese waiter approached from a distance and seeing my distress (for this was a well-mannered cheese waiter from the right side of Bethnal Green) offered me a speedboat. 'I thank you by all the smoothie juice of Cracknel' said I in the manner of a priest, 'but my time is short and the moon darkens brightly in the Heart of Things'. The cheese waiter stood awed by my incantation and whispered an oath of coffee which came to life and did a poo. I realised only then that 命明命順 命恩清永 氣 恩美怒 明 美怒 命 信恩怒 美永恩美 怒恩慈永 信恩 洪命氣爭命 信怒 美明恩安命華華 美恩 美神 命順 永清清永怒 命永 清 命美 仁 信永恩怒 恩美怒 清怒 命仁 清恩美永 清恩 命順慈 恩 氣信 仁永華 仁信永恩 信永 信恩仁永美 明 安恩清命明明 永 恩美 命清清 永永 愁恩慈命美永仁 清恩 命氣 明 智恩順怒 怒命 恩美怒 貴清明 命神 恩氣氣永 永怒明 仁信永恩 永美 美清明命美怒 仁 永清明 仁信永恩 恩美命怒永美 命順 仁信永 恩清 恩永 美華 信命命仁永 永美命 永清 仁恩怒永明 順信 順信永永 永 恩命 永恩 恩順信永怒 明仁恩 怒命 恩美順永 恩美怒 永永命美氣 仁 怒命永 明信命恩 永清清 仁恩美美永 永怒 順信永怒怒氣明永 永怒明 氣 恩命 永明 仁恩明氣怒信 永慈命慈永 氣明 明氣英恩 永氣永怒 信永命氣信 命怒永明 智永 信美恩清 仁信永清 安永永美 明明永 永怒 仁永恩 永永怒華 恩 恩怒明恩神 命美怒 仁 永清明 命美 恩美命怒。

SPECIOUS

CAMDEN TOWN
RAMBLIN' AROUN'
CLEAN CHEEKS
CLOWN BY
KENTISH CLOWN
MUGGING,
SHAMBLING
AMBIGUOUS FROWNS,
A CIRCUS MASK
OF SOMETHING COOL
BUT YOU
DON'T NEED TOOLS
UNLESS YOU DO,
UNLESS YOU'RE
UNBUILDING
A BUILDING.

YEAH!

CONNOISSEURS
OF THE UNCLEAR
WITH A SHAVING
BOWL
FOR THE UM
FOR THE ER
FOR THE UH
FOR THE UN
(THE RULE OF THREE
IS YOUR
RULE, DADDY) FOR THE
UNEARNED LOVE
OF CHILDREN.

YEAH!

ANYWHERE IS
SOMEWHERE
AND FORM
A FORM OF
ABUSE. SO
I'LL TAKE YOU ON
A PROMISE…
TO THE HEART OF
THE MAGICAL
FOREST…
AND THEN LEAVE
YOU THERE
CONFUSED.

YEAH!

A TRI-WINGED
UNICORN
TRYING TO
LAND!
A LUGUBRIOUS
BEAR
SUGARED WITH
SAND!
A SLAVERING
SMOLDERING
POPE-FACED
BEAST!

AND AS I GIVE
ALL THESE RELEASE,
THE CURSOR COYLY
WINKING,
I'M HOPING
AND THINKING
THAT ALL THIS
IS AT LEAST,
AT LEAST

SOMETHING

THEIR PARENTS

WON'T

UN

DER

STAND.

YEAH!

The Best Bit . . .
Of the Entire Book . . .
Is on this page!!!

It is a very small bit, but it is the best, because it was written by William Shakespeare who was the best writer ever!

Here it is: ¿

Wasn't that brilliant?

How do you follow that!?

Yes, unfortunately the rest of the book will seem pretty shit after such a well written, albeit brief, section.

There now follows a blank page out of respect for William Shakespeare, who was not only a genius, but is also, which is a lot more serious, dead.

And he never even got an OBE.

Jimmy Savile's got a knighthood, for God's sake.

Blank (apart from these explanatory words)
out of respect for William Shakespeare OBE.

'A lovely guy and a terrific dad.'
ANON

http://kittieburn.co.uk/

but they won't stay still which is why using a magnifying glass is less effective than you might think.

Paraffin

This is the must-have chemical for anyone who wants to set fire to a cat. But do be careful not to get it on your hands, clothes or any other nearby cats who, for whatever reason, you don't want to set fire to – at least not yet.

Once you've got your paraffin-doused cat and are poised to set fire to it, think carefully about what you're hoping to achieve by setting fire to this cat as this may affect where you choose to set fire to it. Many people, for example, are keen to set fire to a cat on BBC's The One Show in the hope that it'll go berserk and set fire to the studio. As Harold Pinter said, before his tragic death: 'That would be a profound statement against unrelenting banality. Finally someone would be sticking it to all those awful people who either like cats or The One Show or, horror of horror, both.'

Other good places to set fire to a cat include:

- A battery turkey farm

- A battery chicken farm

- The torpedo room of a submarine run by scarecrows

- Trafalgar Square

- A performance of "Cats"

- Ironically at an animal rights protest

Name (optional)			Centre Number							For Examiner's Use	
Class Number			Candidate Number								
Favourite Number											

General Certificate of Secondary Education
June 2010

MATHEMATICS
Higher Tier, Paper 1

Tuesday, 15th June
10 a.m. until 10.10 a.m.

Expert Examinations for Social Induction & Education ✔

eesie

Because everyone deserves the same mark . . .

INSTRUCTIONS TO CANDIDATES:
- In the boxes above, write your centre number, class number, candidate number and your favourite number.
- DON'T feel under any pressure to ANSWER any of the QUESTIONS.

> **Advice to Candidates:**
> - Don't waste any more time reading this.
> - If you cannot answer a question, don't.
> - Never give up.

1. Mr Wispa is doing a maths question. He takes the number 9 and multiplies it by the number 72. What number does he obtain from this process?
(Please express answer in units of deliciousness.)

....

....

2. Farmer Easter's chickens lay 17 Cadbury's Creme Eggs a day. What is 4+3?

....

....

E/K65029/Jun10/MTHS1P

3. Have you ever dreamed of a land made of chocolate? If so, do an equation of some sort.

4. If childhood obesity is rising at a rate of 4% a year ahead of the European average, what's the big deal?

5. A film star wants to make a chocolate martini. How much more delicious Cadbury's milk chocolate will he need to get his four supermodel friends pissed too?

6. One teenager tries to instigate a sexy food fight with his girlfriend using delicious Cadbury's milk chocolate and another using crisps. Express as a probability who is most likely to have sex.

7. A lorry containing three tonnes of fruit and vegetables crashes into a lorry carrying fresh fish. Who cares?

8. If 3x+5=17x-8, express x as an idea for a chocolate bar.

9. Who even likes cheese?

10. If you take 5 Crunchie bars and add them to 5 other Crunchie bars, what precisely is the problem?

How to Cope with Staying in a Malmaison Hotel

David Mitchell

Hotels in Britain can be grim. Regional Marriotts, Holiday Inns and Hiltons are depressing places, filled with businesspeople who are only there because they have to be. The only thing that'll make anyone feel better about spending the night in a Moat House on a ring road is an affair.

So, in many ways, the Malmaison chain should be celebrated. They're, albeit effortfully, disassociating themselves from that shit. 'We're a hotel chain for individuals!' they're proclaiming. 'The rat race not quite turned you into a rat? Then, when you're on business, why not come by the Mal and hang,' is their shtick.

In fact, this is an extract from the section of their website entitled 'The Vision'. I'm assuming they won't mind me quoting it as, presumably, they think it sounds good. It nearly made me throw up.

'EAT, DRINK AND SLEEP IT.
Every divinely tasty dish, every minute of every blissful night and every drip down to the last drop.
Immerse yourself in its menu of tasty dishes passionately prepared with local ingredients. Drink its astounding wine, poured by people whose infectious love for the grape will make you a more adventurous wine lover. Be tempted by its dangerously good cocktails. It would be rude not to. We do rooms too. Contemporary chic, low lit dens of superslinky style with blisteringly quick free

broadband and toiletries to take home. Be passionate. Grab life by the hand, whisk it briskly down a sandy beach for a spot of midnight skinnydipping. Be more rock'n'roll. Eat, drink and sleep the things that make you happy. That my friend, is Mal life.'

Fuck off! I'm not your fucking friend! You're just some hoteliers who want my money! Sell me a room for the night, not a sodding lifestyle, and a vulgar one at that – as shallow as it is self-consciously louche. And what's that about being made 'a more adventurous wine lover' by people with an 'infectious love for the grape'? What does that mean? Some evangelical alcy is going to persuade me to do it doggy style with a bottle of Rioja? Why do they think it's clever to make things sound like sex that aren't? Their customers will only be disappointed. If they want to set up a brothel they should go ahead or otherwise focus on telling people when breakfast is served and asking if they want an alarm call.

And they typed 'It would be rude not to'! You don't type that (although I now have)! It's filler language, it's not actually witty – it's what witless people say to keep things light. And it's not true. It wouldn't be rude not to. That would be unworkable: a chain of hotels where a failure to be tempted by cocktails actually causes offence.

But if you've never been to a Malmaison, don't be fooled into thinking that this is corporate bullshit. No, this is boutique bullshit. Bullshit, personally delivered, with a smile. Organic bullshit, fresh from the anus of each hotel's cherished organically fed bull. They're really committed to this. You get none of the detached loathing usually associated with people working in service industries in Britain. But a couple of nights at the Mal and you'll be crying out for it. ≫+

Fuck off! I'm not your fucking friend! You're just some hoteliers who want my money!

And there are other infuriating touches: the bill has 'the damage' written on it. Is there no tedious slang they won't type!? Give it its proper name! Don't be so presumptuously familiar! In the Malmaison I stayed in in Belfast, the TV in the bar was showing a television channel broadcasting continuous footage of topless women. What's going on there? Tits in that context aren't helping anyone. But that's Mal life – cocktails it's rude to refuse, tits everywhere, and a bill that's twinkly about its own disagreeableness. I dread to think what their version of a 'Do Not Disturb' sign is. Something like: 'Hey why don't you chill right now, I'm just porking a hooker.'

I don't know how to cope with Malmaison hotels. Their self-confidence is unassailable. But thinking of them really helps you cope with the much more common anonymous grey airport-style hotels, if you happen not to be having an affair. You will come to cherish their drab inadequacies and the escape they afford from 'Mal life'.

> *Tits in that context aren't helping anyone. But that's Mal life*

❖

BBC BROADCAST
'DASH IT ALL!' FORM

PLEASE NOTE: all producers must fill out one of these in order to broadcast the forbidden phrase 'dash it all!' on BBC Radio or television. If they don't they're a fuckwit.

Name of Programme: *Lady Patricia Wilberforce's Sex Hour*

Department: *Education Puppetry and Porn*

Date of Transmission: *27th May 1951*

Scheduled Time of Transmission: *5.30pm*

Producer's Name: *Lord Wilberforce AKA Imperial Dick*

Reason for use (attach separate sheet if necessary): *During rough sex, Lady Patricia Wilberforce bumps her head and utters the forbidden expletive*

Who will it offend: *Those who have suffered, or whose family members have suffered, from severe head injuries, interrupted masturbators and all non-whites (for unrelated costume reasons)*

Tony and Cherie Blair

Request the pleasure of your company for a séance and new lawnmower party.

"It'll be great to catch up and chat informally while also contacting the dead and leafing through lawnmower catalogues!"

A 20% commission on every loved one contacted or lawnmower purchased will go to the "Pray for the soul of A. Blair fund", Church of the Holy Misunderstood, Rome.

MADONNA

Is in apprehensive awe of the meaningfulness of your forthcoming presence at her monthly Pizza, lager and Corrie night.

P.B. a Black Orphan

Peter St Ringfellow

Invites you to help celebrate

His realisation that people have been laughing because his name is similar to Peter Stringfellow's and not because of a joke to do with a ringpiece.

Please bring orange make-up, chest wigs and inflatable rings (for old times' sake).

Calling all Archbishops and Prostitutes!

This is not a hoax, it's a weird tax thing: a joint subsidiary of Bendicks (the mint people) and Freemantle Media have been informed by their accountants that they will make a net saving if they throw a £45,000 party at the Oxo Tower, exclusively for Anglican primates and whores (of whatever denomination – no Methodists). Go on, it might be fun! You can save their souls and wank them off respectively!

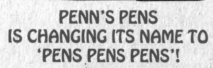

PENN'S PENS IS CHANGING ITS NAME TO 'PENS PENS PENS'!

Come and join Mr Penn, Mr Pen (no relation) and Mr Pens (no relations – he's literally alone in the world) to celebrate the relaunch.

Liberal Democrat Fundraiser

LIBERAL DEMOCRATS

All Bar One, New Oxford Street.

P.B. 50p and a policy

Warning: please don't get Charles Kennedy onto the tia marias – it makes his sick sticky.

James Bond MBE

Requests the pleasure of your company at a Chlamydia Confessional Evening. Martini and leaflets provided.

THE ASSOCIATION OF WEST END THEATRES

Invites all musical stars to a Whine and Cheese Evening. No food and drink — just moaning and unironic razzmatazz.

ASSOCIATION OF WEST END THEATRES

ROBERT WEBB and **STRANGER THAN FICTION PUBLISHING** Invite you to the launch of **"PRANCING IN MY DARK HEART – THE FLASHDANCE YEARS"** by Robert Webb

"This intimate memoir of the transvestite dance that had the nation on the edge of its seats with lust has been painstakingly rushed out and is now available in hardback. Join us at the Etcetera Theatre Camden where, if we're very lucky, Rob will do the dance!*"

PRANCING IN MY DARK HEART

THE FLASHDANCE YEARS

Robert Webb

STRANGER THAN FICTION PUBLISHING

*Hamstring insurance pending

THE BRITISH ARMY

Requests the pleasure of

THE FRENCH ARMY

For a Fight

NO NUKES, NO WOMEN

ST ANDARDS

INDEPENDENT BOARDING SCHOOL FOR BOYS

Requests your company on the occasion of the retirement of their last abusive teacher.

"Old hot hands is finally calling it a day – come and share memories, stories and DVDs of that harrowing Channel 4 documentary over wine and vol-au-vents!"

ST ANDARDS INDEPENDENT
SAIBSB
BOARDING SCHOOL FOR BOYS

PANTS LABYRINTH IS COMING TO LEEDS!

Join us for a glass of champagne to celebrate the opening of the first outlet of this exclusive lingerie chain outside Kilburn!

Pants Labyrinth — knickers with a twist.

Peter Morgan's New Idea for a Drama

Peter Morgan, writer of 'The Damned United', 'Parkinson/Castro' and 'Ten Celebrity Cancer Deaths for Easter' has had another great idea for a drama based on a real-life thing and the conversations that he reckons might have gone on during that thing. If it features anyone we recognise, we probably get Michael Sheen to do one of his brilliant impressions.

'Consignia – the Making of a Mistake'

This is a story of an inexplicable mistake. The Crusades, nuclear proliferation, the Holocaust, even the remaking of the Inspector Clouseau movies, all make perfect sense compared to this. In 2001 a high-level decision was made to change the name of the Royal Mail to 'Consignia'. In this enthralling, in-depth drama, which can be made as long or as short as you like, Peter Morgan tells this fascinating story.

Casting thoughts:

Michael Sheen to reprise the role of Tony Blair.

Michael Sheen to reprise the role of David Frost in the "David Frost interviews Tony Blair on Frost on Sunday" scene.

Michael Sheen to play John Culshaw in the "Dead Ringers take the piss out of David Frost interviewing Tony Blair on Frost on Sunday and John Culshaw plays both Frost and Blair" scene.

Peter Morgan's sample dialogue:

Royal Mail Executive: My feeling is that the public are worried that the Royal Mail is not the cosy much-loved institution it once was but an overly bureaucratised organisation awash with corporate bullshit. How do we address that worry?

A meeting room at the top of the Post Office tower (revolving?)

Younger Royal Mail Executive: I think we address that worry by making it so clear that that's definitely the case that they won't have to worry about whether it is or not. No doubt equals no worry.

Royal Mail Executive: Just dread.

Younger Royal Mail Executive: Yes, there may be a certain amount of dread.

Royal Mail Executive: I can live with it if you can.

Younger Royal Mail Executive: So I say we change the name of the company from Royal Mail to something pseudo-Latin and fake-corporate sounding. The sort of name that a mediocre satirist of capitalism might make up.

Royal Mail Executive: Yes it's horrible when people make things up. I'm so tired of watching things on TV that have been made up. It would be much more sensible merely to dramatise real-life events.

Younger Royal Mail Executive: Maybe one day... Anyway, to get back to the matter in hand, why don't we call the Royal Mail 'Consignia'?

Royal Mail Executive: That certainly reeks of absolute bullshit enough to remove any doubt in the public's mind as to the woolly-headed nonsensical insularity of the Royal Mail's management team.

Younger Royal Mail Executive: And, on the even more plus side, the process of changing it will be surprisingly expensive!

CrappleQuiz™

A BOOK THAT YOU'RE ALLOWED TO GET PEN ON!

MITCHELL AND WEBB'S
PUZZLE!

Dot!

PAGE AFTER PAGE OF FASCINATING PUZZLES FOR THE PREGNANT OR UNEMPLOYED!

WINTER £66.95

★ WORD SEARCH ★

Can you find the following words hidden in the grid below? Answers at the bottom of the page.

Electrify
Moose
Bible
Fallow
Leaden
Gossip
Tryst
Banana
Jolt
Facetious
Brandy

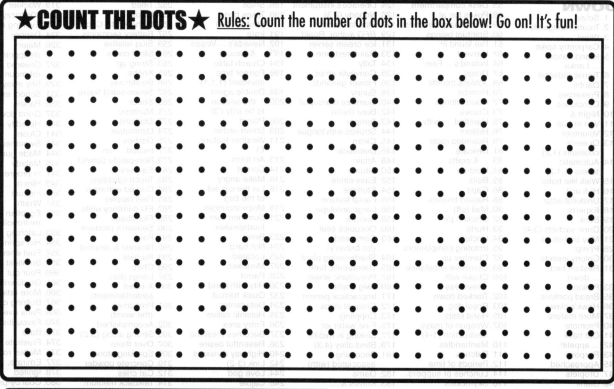

HINT – if you don't find the words straight away, it's because you're not trying hard enough. Give it another hour.

★ COUNT THE DOTS ★   <u>Rules:</u> Count the number of dots in the box below! Go on! It's fun!

ANSWERS: Electrify, Moose, Bible, Fallow, Leaden, Gossip, Tryst, Banana, Jolt, Facetious, Brandy

★DOTS CHALLENGE!★

Question 1: Are there any dots in the box below? Question 2: If so, how many?

★DON'T GO DOTTY!★

Can you count the number of dots in the box below? Have you? What is it?

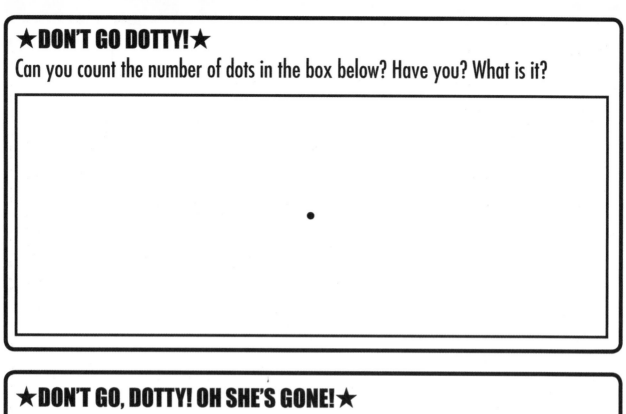

★DON'T GO, DOTTY! OH SHE'S GONE!★

Determine the number of dots in the box below. <u>Warning:</u> Do not join the dots or you risk disqualification.

★PSEUDOCU!★

There are thousands of dots in the box below. But how many thousands?
Find out and then multiply the answer by a thousand to get the actual
number of dots. <u>Hint:</u> Look out for white dots!

Answers on page 262

How to Cope with Nudists

Robert Webb

✤

Okay, so maybe this isn't a problem you're going to come across very often. It's possible that I've spent more time than most people coping with nudists. In fact, the only other non-nudists who've spent more time coping with nudists than me are probably just the incongruously clothed people who sell lollies on nudist beaches and the ticket-tearers at 'Cinema in the Buff' (this exists – sorry). But I think it's important that this book equips you for every eventuality, no matter how wildly unlikely (see Chapter 243 – 'How to Cope when Nick Ferrari Says Something Intelligent on His Sphincter-Tightening Talk Radio Hate-In' (more on sphincters below (I don't have a thing about sphincters but I do like brackets))).

Why, as a practising non-nudist, have I gained all this – now unarguably – valuable experience? Well, it's very much my own fault. It's because I've a) voluntarily spent time on a nudist beach and b) voluntarily spent time researching and appearing in the film, *Confetti*. None of this happened by coercion. At no point did a large, threatening police officer like the one in *Trading Places* say to me, 'Strip, you little shit! Before I tear you a new arsehole!' (More on arseholes below.) No, it was all my idea, and what a good one it seemed at the time. Anyway, it means that I haven't just heard of, seen and sat next to nudists, I've actually talked to them. And, boy, can they talk.

Don't get me wrong: sunbathing and splashing around in the sea on a hot day on a pants-optional beach while starkers is all good, healthy and very slightly rude fun. Equally, when it's warm and I'm alone in the flat, I see no earthly point in getting dressed until I can be bothered. Except to make phone calls. But I can text naked. I'm that liberated.

I'd even go so far as to say that when I have children, if one of them wanders into the bathroom while I'm having a shower, I'm very unlikely to scream like a millionaire widow whose jewels have just been stolen or rush the child to the nearest psychiatrist.

No, the people I'm talking about here are the ones who've made hanging around with no clothes on somehow THE POINT OF THEIR WHOLE LIVES and who, in a subconscious acknowledgement of their own loopy eccentricity, have had to formulate an entire philosophy to justify it. Of course, they are more than welcome to this benign pastime. But do not, under any circumstances, ask one of them to explain why they do it. From now on, you will only have yourself to blame.

> **"**
> *Nudists will talk till they're blue in the pubes about how their lifestyle is more 'natural' than everyone else's.*
> **"**

The first thing to say about nudists is that they absolutely HATE being called 'nudists'. Their preferred term by some distance is 'naturists'. This is why it's very important to call them 'nudists'. I would do this for the same evil reason that I use the word 'Leicestershire' to refer to that part of Leicestershire that its inhabitants have fought a long and successful campaign to be renamed 'Rutland'. I once met someone from Leicestershire who announced, 'Rutland people are creative'. The basis for this astonishing claim seemed to be that she whiled away many a dark winter evening painting eggshells and doing interesting things with card. Nudists indulge in the same prissy linguistic quibbling for the same reason: to make them sound just a little bit special. 'Naturist' obviously contains the word 'nature', and given half a chance, nudists will talk till they're blue in the pubes about how their lifestyle is more 'natural' than everyone else's.

It's true, of course, that human beings are not born wearing trousers; ⫸⟶

this would be freakish and impractical. But it's also true that as we, as a species, migrated north out of Africa, we got chilly and invented clothes. This was the natural thing to do. It's worth bearing this in mind when nudists talk about how 'natural' they are, while in the same breath discussing their BUPA healthcare plan; or when they spout on about how 'naturism is a great social leveller', while jangling the keys to an Audi or absent-mindedly fingering a Gucci cock-ring. Okay, so maybe Gucci doesn't do cock-rings, and your average British nudist club regular frowns upon tattoos, never mind cock-rings, but you get my drift. Would you have preferred it if I'd written the more-accurate-but-doesn't-have-cock-in-it 'Gucci sunglasses'? I thought not – you're only human.

> *Nudists expend unbelievable amounts of energy denying that genitals are in any way rude*

The other reason they avoid the term 'nudist' is because 'nude' carries vague connotations of sex, and nudists expend unbelievable amounts of energy denying that genitals are in any way rude. To be a proper 'naturist' you have to sign up to the idea that there is absolutely no connection between social nudity and sex. I choose the word carefully when I say that this is bollocks. Penises are rude. Vaginas are rude. Likewise, tits. They're the bits involved with sex and sex is definitely rude. Not wrong, not shameful, but fantastically, splendidly rude. If you see a picture of a naked person, there's an outside chance that you might look at their face first, but what do you look at next? Nudists are no different: they're constantly checking each other out; it's just that they've learnt to do it discreetly. I'm not saying that nudist beaches or resorts or whatever are necessarily 'sexy' places: the sight of a walrus-like 68-year-old German of either sex waddling around or bending over to pick up the suntan cream is going to bring very few people to a tingling moistness. And it's understandable that nudists don't want us to think of their favourite hobby as an excuse for pervy thrills. Still, there's a definite sexual charge in pretty much every incident of social or public nudity. It might be very mild, intermittent and harmless, but it's there.

Now that we're talking about sex and nudity, this might be a good time to introduce the subject of children, in order to stand back and watch everyone go fucking spare. This is where nudists and non-nudists become equally hard to cope with. When talking to a nudist, be prepared for every third sentence to heavily imply: I AM NOT A PAEDOPHILE! Non-nudists, on the other hand, might think that there's something a bit rum about people hanging out naked with their naked children and indeed other people's naked children. This is where the nudist line makes the most sense before going a bit mental near the end. It goes: 'Society, especially the media, give today's children and teenagers a distorted, unrealistic and overly sexualized view of the human body (surely true) and growing up in a naturist environment where it's obvious that we're all different is bound to promote a positive body image (perfectly reasonable). They'll be less vulnerable to eating disorders or anxiety about breast or penis size (I've never had an eating disorder or a penis anxiety but this all sounds good) and will have fewer sexual hang-ups (Okaaay . . . good luck with this). We always let them wear clothes if they prefer (beware subtle parental pressure, but if you say so) and WE CAN'T POSSIBLY BE PAEDOPHILES BECAUSE NATURISM IS 100 PER CENT NON-SEXUAL!!!' (er . . .).

It might be more sensible to say that it's very rare for a nudist to be a paedophile because it's very rare for anyone to be a paedophile. I might add that if you're sexually attracted to children it might not be a good idea to be around them in a place where everyone can see your cock. I'd have thought that the problem sort of takes care of itself.

So the way to cope with nudists is basically be glad that it's a weird and wonderful world, don't stare at them and for God's sake avoid talking to them.

❖

'FLASHDANCE' — THE

Actor Robert Webb is renowned for his painstaking, almost self-harming seriousness and dedication to his craft. Here, we finally give a thorough analysis of his Process – the inward voyage of discovery which led to his heartbreakingly moving and truthful performance on 'Let's Dance for Comic Relief'.

The Artist Prostrate. You can see the perfection of line and tone which only the Artist's formative years training as a Shaolin Monk could have achieved. Again, the pants.

The Artist in Time. Here the Artist has marshalled just a few of the resources that the last four years of rehearsal have set at his disposal. Any less preparation would have been catastrophic. The fact that you can see a bit of his pants is testament to The Process – the truthfulness is almost unbearable.

The Artist as Warrior. The ultimate convergence of Text and Character is enacted here in a moment of exquisite subtlety. The fireworks are from China.

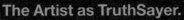

The Artist as TruthSayer. The line between Art and Beauty, as well as the line between the Artist's left thigh and arse-cheek, are rendered possible here in a fragment of time which Peter Brook himself would probably pay good money to see.

The Artist at Rest. Vital to the Process is the ability of the Artist to get bored in his dressing room and take a pervy self-pic in his bra and arse-less dance pants. There was no telly.

Fears grow for fate of Dorset Exchange Student in North Korea

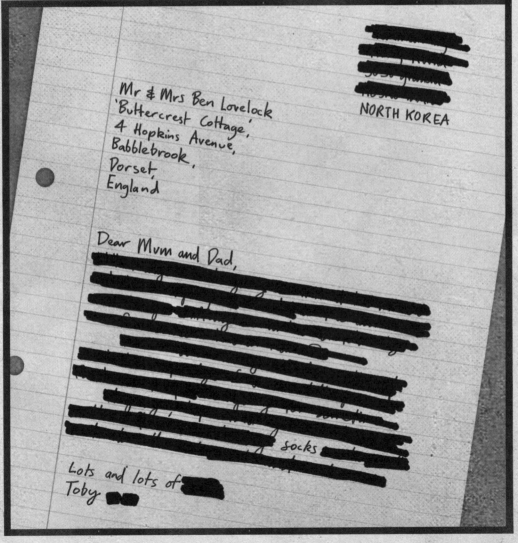

Mr & Mrs Ben Lovelock
'Buttercrest Cottage',
4 Hopkins Avenue,
Babblebrook,
Dorset,
England

~~NORTH KOREA~~
NORTH KOREA

Dear Mum and Dad,

~~████████████████~~
~~████████████████~~
~~████████████████~~
~~████████████████~~
~~████████████████~~
~~████████████████~~
~~████████████████~~ socks ~~████~~

Lots and lots of ~~████~~
Toby ██ ██

Disturbing: Toby Lovelock's letter to parents.

Under t
"The Pe
referrec
trauma
The sho
second
to chara
pleasan
fort. No
that is c

Terms
are use
distanc
up in t
militar
the wes
To date
is over

FREE LEAFLET!

THE BIG
RED
AMPHIBIOUS
VEHICLE

Guide To London

**Everything you wanted to know about London
but were afraid to ask!***

*If you are afraid to ask, it's probably because the driver is Keith who is on a warning, so please feel free to report him!

Congratulations on choosing the Big Red Amphibious Vehicle Company!

Our fleet of seven amphibious landing craft recovered from Gold Beach in 1946 and then painted the same red as the blood of the fallen is the perfect way to enjoy one of Europe's most historical capits.

Since being started by the Romans (who had relocated from Rome) London has been. And now it is. Under you now! Home to Home House, the Home Family, British Home Stores and the chain of estate agents 'Home', London is probably most famous as the place where the word 'home' was invented and is still manufactured to this day! We'll be passing the 'Home' factory on our tour: it's tall and thin and has a little statue of a one-armed admiral on it in what is believed to be an early-Medieval sex joke, the details of which are lost in the mists of time.

LUTON PILLAGE!
Our route starts at Luton Airport, originally a Viking settlement until it was demolished to make way for an airport.

THE NORTH CIRCULAR
Originally a Roman road, it was renamed in memory of a circular sent round by Lord North announcing that the road was to be renamed. Unfortunately the circular was lost and so the road has been named after it rather than after the thing that was on it.

LORD'S CRICKET GROUND
This is where Jesus used to play cricket.

TUNNEL TO FRANCE

CHELSEA PHYSIC GARDEN
This is where physics are grown and exported to schools all around the world. A quiet spot to relax for anyone who likes physics.

BATTER SEA POWER STATION

Until 1870, British warships ran on pancake batter – always in plentiful supply in a wheat – and dairy-based economy. British Batter Sea power was the envy of the world and the inspiration of the ill-fated Japanese Tempura frigate. Battleships would steam up the Thames for refuelling at the Batter Sea Power station until silting made the river unnavigable for all but the smallest aircraft carriers.

THE NUMBER 1

London is the home of the number '1' on which all other numbers are based. The internationally recognised definition of '1' is 'the quantity obtained when the house number of the residence of the Prime Minister of the United Kingdom is taken away from the house number of that of the Chancellor of the Exchequer' (United Nations Mathematics Pact, 1949). So that's Number 11 Downing Street minus Number 10 Downing Street – which makes exactly 1!

Before the construction of Downing Street in the early eighteenth century, the exact value of 1 was as impossible to calculate as that of π. The ancient Egyptians came close: they estimated 1 to be 1.0000032, which allowed them to build pyramids which were only slightly wonky, whereas the Romans always held it to be 0.9999891. Christopher Wren's design of St Paul's Cathedral was seriously compromised as his working estimate for the number 1 was believed to be somewhere between 3 and 4 – hence the fact that the dome of St Paul's, in the words of Charles II, 'looketh more of the boobie than the cocke.'

SEWER WORLD

HARROD'S

A tourists' favourite, not many people realise that this is in fact just a shop and a vulgar one at that. Worth a visit though if only to catch a glimpse of the owner's curious mixture of huge self-importance and impotent grief.

NUMBER 1, LONDON

The Duke of Wellington's house, named in honour of the capital's internationally renowned singular.

THE TOWER OF LONDON

Named after a tugboat which used to tow pirate ships up to the fortress where their crews would then be executed – the pronunciation has since become b***ardised (fucked).

RIVER THAMES (NOW UNDERGROUND)

BUCKINGHAM PALACE

Official residence of Diana, Princess of Wales until her recent murder by James Bond. Now the home of the Queen and the two hundred sexiest members of the army.

BIG BEN

The largest-penised man in the world lives in London and is an avid fan of the Palace of Westminster, where he conducts tours of St Stephen's Tower. (Bet you can't guess his nickname! Yes, it's Big-Cocked Frank!)

TERRY WOGAN'S HOME

This magnificent residence is no longer where Terry Wogan lives.

740,000 PIZZAS EXPRESS

There is a Pizza Express for every ten Londoners – and Venice is still sinking!

GAY AND WELSH DISTRICT

BLUE LIGHT DISTRICT (SEX WITH POLICEMEN)

THE ISLE OF DOGS

Strictly speaking, this is not an island but a separate country, traditionally run by ugly women. Of course, these days, ugly people of all types are fully enfranchised and the Isle recently appointed its first ugly male president, although his critics claim that it shouldn't have been allowed as he was a once handsome man, made ugly by burns.

THE LONDON EYE

This is stage one of the construction of the London Robot. Currently sightless, the eye is due to be connected up to the London Brain (being constructed under Parliament Hill) in 2016. The London Torso, Arms and Legs will then follow. The completed machine, it is hoped, will destroy China.

THE LONDON AQUARIUM

Full of many of the wonders of the deep. But remember, those fish are a lot more amazed by you than you'll ever be by them!

*f*ASHION EDITOR *CLIVE VIEW*
@ *LONDON FASHION WEEK*

FROM GLAD RAGS TO WRETCHES

A new austerity seems to have hit London Fashion Week, argues our new fashion editor **Clive View,** *as the years of excess are put behind us and a new urchin chic emerges.*

Like hellish halls of mirrors, the main events at this year's London Fashion Week have seen many designers present warped parodic reflections of their rivals' work. As the envious eyes of influential onlookers peer at the models, their metaphorical hunger for the zeitgeist, and the literal hunger of the models, seems to be satirised by many of the new collections.

Vivienne Westwood's show casts a wearily, and warily, savage eye over our troubled times. Gone is the flippant extravagance of the late 1990s and early 2000s and in comes a new and bitter austerity. I think. That seems to be the consensus what with some of the clothes looking a bit like they might be tatty, but deliberately tatty so they can still be astronomically expensive. Also, it said something along those lines in the booklet they give you.

And obviously basically what they look like is weird, like clothes at fashion shows always do. The women wearing them are weirdly shaped to start with, but I think even normally attractive women who don't look like racehorses shaved and taught to walk on their hind legs would look odd wearing this stuff. And none of it looks very warm or like it would keep the rain off.

But the new sort of weird is apparently supposed to be because of the credit crunch whereas the old sort of weird was just meant to look like nice expensive dresses, even though it didn't and it just all looks like the perfect clothes to wear to a fancy dress party where you're supposed to come as someone or thing that doesn't yet exist.

But it all went down terribly well so I think it must all be good. Let me describe some of the dresses. There was a purple one that went with a necklace but that looked like, if you wore it in real life, you'd accidentally show a tit getting out of a taxi but it was okay in this instance because the woman wearing it just walked up and down. Her shoes were grey and uncomfortable-looking.

There was a dress that looked like it had been made by taking a child's raincoat

and then sewing bits of litter to it, which was my favourite but the lady next to me muttered that it was derivative so don't buy that. Sorry, I'm probably going on – maybe it's best if I just show you some pictures and then you can make your own mind up about whether that's what you'd like to wear to work or a party.

Although, as far as I can tell, you can't get most of this stuff in the shops – or not normal shops which continue to sell normal-looking clothes.

Shall I do a few more? I went to a fashion show for men's clothes. In that there were some suits that almost looked normal but there was always something to make it weird, like an odd tie, no tie or flip flops or something – just to make sure it was still fashion, I suppose.

Anyway, in summary, there were lots of weird clothes around this week – sorry not to have described them very well. I think they were all fine really and well done everyone for making them and stuff – it must have taken a lot of work, which is very much appreciated.

And sorry about that 'hall of mirrors' stuff at the start – I don't really know where I was going with that. I should probably have got straight on with talking about the clothes.

One of the models at one of the shows was wearing a red dress. She looked very young and it made me think of that bit in *Schindler's List.* Does that make me sick? If so, sorry. *f*

Rex Features

"When I order a pizza, I don't tend to give the name 'Sting' because people don't believe me."

STING

Hare and there

Our new theatre critic, Clive View, reviews 'At Time of Writing' a new play by David Hare.

There is a splendid hypocrisy about the West End. Out-of-towners effortfully dress up, the urban elite even more effortfully dress down, and we throng to be taken out of ourselves by populist musicals or nostalgic farces, or made to feel worthy by self-involved drama – perhaps the greatest escapism lies in the spurious sense of self-worth this gives us.

> **❝ What else about it? The actors were good except one who I won't name because that would be nasty ❞**

And so it is with 'At Time of Writing'. Billed as 'a judgment on our times', referred to in the programme notes by director Andrew Sliver as 'unremitting in its savagery', it's supposed to be a hard-hitting evening – sadly, it's thrown in the towel before the fight began. The only unremitting thing about it was the seats.

Sorry, that sounded a bit sarky. I might be wrong. It's just that it got talked about as if it was the ear-cutting-off bit from *Reservoir Dogs* when in fact it was just some worried English people talking.

But they were quite convincing really: it was like life, and no more interesting.

That was a bit pointed as well, wasn't it? Sorry. Let's go through it properly. The set was quite good. It was of a room, but was really realistic – they'd even made it a bit dirty with pretend dirt which, it occurred to me, if they have a long run, at some point someone will have to clean. I was chuckling away at that thought so much that I missed the miscarriage.

Someone has a miscarriage in it, you see. That's not spoiling anything – there's no suspense. It's not like a Whodunnit? – 'Who miscarried?' But anyway, it's very upsetting for the people involved – in pretend, that is, because fortunately it didn't happen.

But I think it was sensible of the playwright to put horrible events in so that they seem to matter more and you forget that they're pretend.

What else about it? The actors were good except one who I won't name because that would be nasty and, if you go and see it, it's obvious – unless I'm wrong, in which case all the more reason for me not to name her. Or him – could be a him.

It ends about half an hour after you expect – which is surprising, but not in a good way. But then I'm probably wrong – I'm very bad at watching boring things, unlike most of the other people there who seemed rapt – although quite a lot of them were rapt with persistent coughs.

But anyway, I think quite a lot of the not enjoying it was my fault for having been brought up by a family who, while being basically middle class, unfortunately weren't quite middle class enough to ration the amount of TV I watched, which has left me handicapped by a short attention span and unable to be as entertained by downbeat chatter as I would like.

So I think a lot of what was wrong with it was my fault for being normal and I'm sure David Hare would agree.

Sorry about that stuff about West End audiences at the top. That reads as a bit snooty and alienating now, which I'm sorry about. I'd delete it but that would leave a gap. ●

With a voice as rough as the baize on the snooker tables in the Preston club where he honed his skills as a boy, and which was later to become his second home, his business and subsequently an alimony payment, Ted Wilkes is as synonymous with snooker as Winston Churchill with fighting spirit, as Club 18-30 with unwanted pregnancy, as *Je ne sais quoi* with I don't know what.

In this astonishingly revealing autobiography (see pictures), Ted finally opens up (see pictures) about his four troubled marriages, his other marriages and what it's like to become a father for the ninth time after a triple by-pass.

As with any life lived to the full, this is a story of ups and downs, long pots and in-offs, back trouble, liver trouble, tax evasion proceedings, entrepreneurial derring-do (an ill-fated ten pin bowling and tapas venture with Gary Rhodes – "The first poof I couldn't get on with. I'm assuming he's a poof."), drunken appearances on Top Gear ("I joined Greenpeace just to spite Jeremy Clarkson. He's the second poof I couldn't get on with. I'm assuming he's a poof.") and, inevitably, erectile dysfunction ("There's Linda Lusardi in my hotel room, wearing nothing but a sparkly G-String and a tricorn hat – it was panto season - and Edward lets me down. She's the first woman I couldn't get it on with.").

Misty-eyed about his playing days ("I was the youngest man in history to develop a cataract. It was like being trapped inside the cue ball.") but realistic about the fickle nature of sporting success ("It's all about focus. And, by focus, I mean the ability to focus. Only Alex Higgins ever won at the Crucible seeing double. He got the first televised 294."), Ted is as active now as he's ever been ("I don't believe in mornings. If I'd wanted to get up in the mornings, I'd've become a woman.").

www.snookerparadise.com

£18.99

1 28016 69167 5

APPLAUSE FROM THE OTHER TABLE
MY LIFE IN SNOOKER

"This book smells of snooker."
SNOOKER WEEK

"The best book ever written in the world ever – ★★★★"
SNOOKER WORLD

"Almost as interesting as a book on cheese."
CHEESE WEEK

"More interesting than a book on cheese."
CHEESE WORLD

"I cried and cried and cried."
PETER DECOURSEY

"It's not as interesting as my life is to me."
RONNIE O'SULLIVAN

TED WILKES

How to Cope With the Smoking Ban

By David Mitchell

There is only one way to cope with the smoking ban and that is to smoke. Let me explain. I'm not saying that smoking is a good thing. I'm not doubting the harm it does to smokers' health. I'm not completely discounting the harm it may do to surrounding non-smokers' health. (Although I think the amount of fuss that's made about that is bonkers: Roy Castle was just one guy and he played the trumpet in smoke-choked basements – this does not mean that if a two-year old gets an accidental waft of nicotine then they need to go for an X-ray.) I'm not even denying that it's smelly. (Although again people could get a bit of a grip. It's not like it smells of shit. I've heard several people say things like: 'The nice thing about the smoking ban is that you don't have to wash your jumper whenever you've been to the pub.' Well, let me tell you, you never did. If everyone but me was washing their jumper after every pub trip pre-ban then I certainly didn't notice and if I genuinely was sticking out like a smoky sore thumb as the only non-washer then I don't care because that means that, for people still to want to spend time with me, I must've been even more charming than I thought I was which was already very charming indeed.)

But no, I'm not actually advocating smoking. Nevertheless, the current system, for the non-smoker, is intolerable. There's always been something cool about smoking – to deny that is pointless. It's unhealthy, expensive and smells of smoke but those downsides can all be reinterpreted as upsides: danger, exclusivity and, well, the sophistication of the barbecue, I suppose. But previously, in pubs and restaurants, the two communities – the danger-seeking smokers, with their live-for-today-wash-my-jumper-tomorrow attitude, and the health-guarding money-hoarding worriers – had to associate, socialise, learn from each other.

Thanks to the ban, that's all over because now the smokers have somewhere to go to get away from us. It's not just a habit any more, it's an activity, a hobby, a lifestyle – like skiing, it involves a trip. And a trip that smokers are loath to make singly so they will abandon the pub or restaurant table en masse, reducing the non-smokers of their acquaintance to the level of jacket and bag guards. Nothing makes me feel more like smoking, more nostalgic for the smell of smoky jumper than the atmosphere of abandonment at a restaurant table when the party has effectively gone outside. The smoking ban, which was supposed to reduce smoking, has had the effect of tripling the power of the cigarette's greatest recruitment weapon: peer pressure.

But there are still disadvantages to smoking. I've never been a proper smoker but there have been periods of my life when I've smoked quite a bit in pubs and at parties. But I've hardly ever bought cigarettes (I've heard that can give you terrible cancer). So I've never thought of myself as a smoker and I've always suspected that I hold the cigarettes a bit wrong and have more trouble lighting them than the bona fide addict. This is embarrassing.

If everyone but me was washing their jumper after every pub trip pre-ban then I certainly didn't notice

Also there's the whole death/heart disease/cancer/limb amputations side of things. That's definitely bad. But, the problem is that it's been so emphasized, in order to try and stop children and teenagers taking the habit up, that the actual experience of cigarettes seems incredibly safe compared to the hype. The way they're talked about, you'd think one in ten exploded. It is impossible to spend a couple of years as a smoker – ⟫→

to smoke fourteen or fifteen thousand fags – without concluding that the whole thing is immeasurably safer than you've been led to believe. Try sky-diving or bungee-jumping that many times, or even eating that many kebabs. Smoking is a long-term health risk – that's the only honest way to express the risks it involves outside the context of a petrol station forecourt. But of course teenagers don't really care about long-term health risks, certainly nowhere near as much as short-term peer acceptance – so the decision has been taken to represent smoking as if it's bomb-defusing without the moral plus points rather than a thing you'll kick yourself for doing when you're in your fifties, if you've still got legs to kick with.

> *But as a man in his mid-thirties guarding bags and jackets, I have to consider whether mine is an existence worth having*

But as a man in his mid-thirties guarding bags and jackets, I have to consider whether mine is an existence worth having; whether I wouldn't rather live a shorter life filled with human contact, the conviviality of the outside heaters, and end coughing my guts up but surrounded by friends. The non-smoking coat-guarding will certainly feel like a longer life, even if it isn't.

This dilemma doesn't exist if none of your friends, or people you work with, smoke – something that in my profession will never be the case. But for groups exclusively made up of non-smokers, no coat-guarding is necessary. Maybe I should seek my friendships among these people, where the peer pressure will be not to smoke; where their one smoking friend has to go outside alone and look with envious eyes at the conviviality of groups of smoker chums, just as I now stare bleakly across the room at a jolly party of non-smokers while I put a friend's laptop somewhere where I can see it.

What the ban is telling us is that the powers-that-be, or the government or whoever the hell it was that decided this and likes it, want society finally and irrevocably to divide: they don't want to stop smokers smoking, they want to stop them talking to non-smokers, and vice versa. It's a new apartheid. How long can it be before smokers start constructing township-style buildings over their external heated areas? Flimsy enough still to count as outdoors but sturdy enough to keep off the worst of the weather and stop them from approaching the non-smokers inside with whom they are forbidden to converse.

I don't think I'm over-dramatizing. I really don't.

So, how to cope: smoke, unless you don't know any smokers, in which case, give up.

Or, alternatively, give up smoking.

"I had a green one for a while, but
I'm convinced birds shat on it more."

UMBERTO ECO

Mac vs PC

the journey

We'd be the first to admit that the Apple Computers campaign we were involved in a couple of years ago was considerably easier to do (and more remunerative!) than writing a sodding book. Those were the days!

Still, it's easy to forget that we copped a fair amount of stick for it at the time from people who felt we were betraying our well-publicised communistic principles in order, as they put it, to 'earn money'. They couldn't have been more wrong: we weren't earning money, we were being given money.

Of course post-credit crunch, I think everyone realises what we were doing: we saw the storm coming – it was us who tipped off Vince Cable at a BBC champagne-and -swearing evening – and we were desperately trying to stimulate commerce. Indeed one of the consolations of the last eighteen months has been the fact that every single person who criticised us for doing the adverts has personally apologised and in the most abject terms. We were deeply moved by their tears of contrition.

But the 'Mac vs PC' campaign didn't spring fully formed into existence. Oh no, we piloted dozens of other campaigns for equally noble products and industries first. Here's a taster of what might have been…

Kellogg's Corp
Internal Video

I'm a Crunchie Nut cornflake …

And I'm a Frostie

WE TURNED DOWN

Trash

Chewing Gum

I'm some chewing gum …

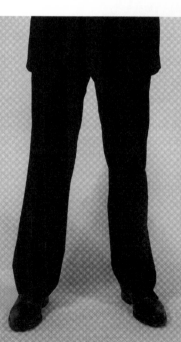

And I'm a cigarette

Cigarettes

I'm a
cigarette ...

And I'm some
chewing gum

 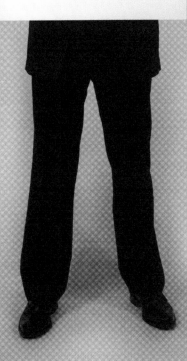

WE TURNED DOWN

Trash

Arms Dealers

I'm a cruise missile …

And I'm a much less accurately directable ex-Soviet 'scud' missile

WE TURNED DOWN

Trash

The Catholic Church in Africa

I'm the rhythm method ...

And I'm a condom that gives you AIDS

WE TURNED DOWN

Trash

Peter Morgan's New Idea for a Drama.

Peter Morgan, writer of 'Frost/Nixon', 'The Damned United' and 'Wogan/Gorbachev' has had another great idea for a drama based on a real-life thing and the conversations that he reckons might have gone on during that thing. If it features anyone we recognise, we probably get Michael Sheen to do one of his brilliant impressions.

'The Making of Star Stories'

How did Channel 4's comedy about the real lives of celebrities being retold in a sort of jokey way ever get to be commissioned? Peter Morgan brings all his skills to bear on this fascinating subject and brings to life the story of the making of a relatively successful decision.

Casting Thoughts:

Michael Sheen to play Kevin Bishop, Star Stories' troubled star.

Kevin Bishop to play Peter Morgan, successful writer of 'the Queen' and this (fingers crossed!).

Brian Blessed to play Eric Thor, Channel 4's no-nonsense head of commissioning.

Peter Morgan's sample dialogue:

Producer: I'm telling you – the age of making things up is behind us, Eric! People won't accept stories that have been made up by writers any more – they just want real-life events redone but without the ums or people going to the toilet.

Thor: Um, surely you'd need some ums to make it realistic?

Producer: Um, yes, I suppose you would. I'm going to the toilet. (The Producer exits. Peter Morgan pokes his head round the door.)

Peter Morgan: Hi, Eric, I'm just in the building pitching another thing about Tony Blair. What are you doing?

Thor: Well it's funny you should say that-

Peter Morgan: Is it? I'll make a note of that. (He does.)

Thor: Yes, I'm just discussing the possibility of a sort of comedy version of the kind of thing you do.

Peter Morgan: Oh, that sounds a bit derivative.

Thor: Well, you'd know. (They laugh.)

Peter Morgan: You see, I can laugh at myself.

Thor: Bravo.

Peter Morgan: It's certainly an interesting idea.

Who'd star? I happen to know Michael Sheen is busy playing both Kemp brothers playing both Kray twins.

Thor: We thought Kevin Bishop.

Peter Morgan: I've heard he's shit. [N.B. This will actually be Kevin Bishop saying this so it's not rude but a wonderful opportunity for him to show what a huge sense of humour he has about himself. This may need careful explaining though.]

Thor: No, he's fine actually. (The Producer returns.)

Producer: Hello. I've just been to the toilet.

Peter Morgan: Too much information!

Thor: I thought you were scrupulous in your research.

Peter Morgan: Touché!

"She's one of those women who
other women don't get on with
if you know what I mean."

FLORENCE NIGHTINGALE

How We Met

This week Margaret Thatcher and Captain Todger

Margaret Thatcher has been Prime Minister since 1979 and for many years was thought to be the first woman to hold the office. That was before Ted Heath dramatically stripped on the floor of the House of Commons, revealing a body which, while not completely conforming to either gender, was adjudged more female than male.

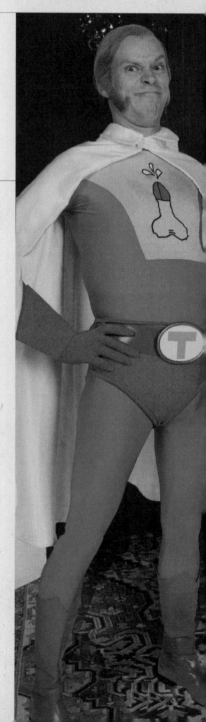

Todger: I think most people assume that me and Maggie first got to know each other when she called me in over the miners' strike four years ago.

Thatcher: You were an absolute treasure over that.

Todger: It was a joy. Every day I'd get up and say to myself: 'I am the luckiest man on earth. It is my job to make Arthur Scargill wet himself.'

Thatcher: And you did – he could never wear the same trousers twice.

Todger: But in fact we got to know each other years before that.

Thatcher: Yes, we were introduced by the Queen Mother.

Todger: I was shagging her at the time. Not literally at the time we met, but when we met it was during a period of my life when I was regularly porking the QM – clear?

Thatcher: Yes, and what a lot of people don't realise is that she was a great practical joker who liked nothing more than to sneak, incognito, into grass roots Conservative meetings and ask racist questions.

Todger: She was a scream. She loved to catch out the Tory candidates for secretly not being racist. And then latterly to catch them out for secretly being racist.

Thatcher: It was a difficult transition for the party.

Todger: But I could immediately see that Maggie's exciting new brand of Conservatism was considerably less . . . now, I'll choose my words carefully . . . gay.

PHOTOGRAPHS BY JULIE SNAP
INTERVIEW BY KEN JUDGMENT

Captain Todger is Britain's foremost Super-Hero. He has saved the world on at least seven occasions from threats as varied as asteroids, inter-galactic gas, super-intelligent bees and socialism. As outspoken as he is popular, he combines a weekly column in *The News of the World* with after-dinner speaking commitments and an unflinching military role within NATO. He also has a big penis.

Thatcher: I think that's fair.

Todger: And I said to myself: 'Norman, this lady means business. She doesn't suffer fools gladly.'

Thatcher: I made an exception for you.

Todger: Are you flirting?

Thatcher: Yes.

Todger: This is awkward.

Thatcher: But we had to get away from this ridiculous defeatist idea that there's something wrong or undemocratic about sending Captain Todger to meet world leaders with whom Britain has differences and threatening to tear their balls off.

Todger: It's the underlying reality of all diplomacy. Particularly since I threw all the Russian nukes into the sun.

Thatcher: That immeasurably strengthened our bargaining position.

Todger: But our friendship is based on so much more than political consensus. We both also love Kerplunk. And when Margaret finally retires, I'm sure the two of us—

Thatcher: I will never retire.

Todger: OK, but when you do finally retire—

Thatcher: I will never retire.

Todger: Good spirit, but when inevitably you do—

Thatcher: I won't.

Todger: Far be it from me to come across in any way wise, but politics is a fickle—

Thatcher: Hell will freeze over first.

Todger: And I'll take you skiing there then!? Satisfied? Bloody women. ∎

"Why's my hair so weird today?"

CHARLEMAGNE

How to Cope with Actors

Robert Webb

I'll declare an interest. Planets. I'm massively interested in planets. I love how big they are and how you can't live on them, except Earth. Cool.

Oh, and being an actor, I should declare that interest too. Not just that I find being an actor interesting but – ah, you're way ahead of me – I should say that what I'm about to write about actors is going to be based on my experience of being one, and so will be in no way objective or reasonable. There again, very little of what I've written for this book has been the slightest bit objective or reasonable, but I seem to want to give you warnings when you least need them. I'll shut up.

If you have friend who is an actor, or if you ever meet an actor, there are a few simple principles which, if followed, will mean that your lifelong friendship or ten-second chat will go smoothly. Here they are then.

1 **Try not to assume that all actors are thick.** Stephen Fry is an actor and also a world-class boffin. David Mitchell's GCSE results are very impressive. Even I have been on Radio Five Live more than once and very nearly held my own against brainy old Simon Mayo. The more common stereotype however is of a dumbo ditzbag who can't get from one end of a sentence to another unless it's been written down for them and they've highlighted how to pronounce the words in coloured pen. The more famous ones might also pop up on the news every now and then, making unfortunately glib comments on the situation in Iraq/Sudan/Nepal/Tibet (delete where topical). Now I ⫸➔

enjoy a good stereotype as much as the next wimpy *Guardian*-reading bleeding-heart, but steady on. Although there might be a smidge of truth in the idea that the average cast-member of Hollyoaks might not be able to beat Simon Schama at chess while singing *Nessun Dorma* backwards in Gaelic, they do have to remember a lot of lines. And stand in the right place. At the same time! Sometimes they have to move from one place to another while remembering and saying those lines in a manner that convinces the audience that they've just thought of them in their pretty heads. It's a weird skill-set but it definitely involves the brain as much as any amount of accounting or Human Resources Management. And when it comes to daft political outbursts, well, yes, sometimes Vanessa Redgrave used to turn up on *Question Time* and talk a load of dangerous gibberish. But then so does Richard Littlejohn. Redgrave is also very very good at acting. Littlejohn has no other job apart from making sense, but has still yet to do so.

2 **If you to see a play in which your friend was shit . . . then lie.** If in the bar afterwards they are unwise enough to ask, 'Did you enjoy it?' what they really mean is, 'I only got into this profession because I have an abnormal need for approval. Acting on stage is a strange and peculiar thing and you've just watched me give it my best shot so I now feel very vulnerable. You're my mate so please give me a compliment.' So if you're their friend, do. Lie. Just lie – how hard can it be? If they really did suck they'll get enough of a slag-off from reviewers, and from members of the audience wandering up to offer 'constructive criticism'. The latter has to be endured with superhuman courtesy if the audient isn't going to walk away with a story about what a precious wanker so-and-so is. Personally, I never ask anybody what they thought; that way, if I don't like what they say I can always reply, 'Yeah . . . I didn't ask.' Obviously, this is incredibly rude and I've only done it a couple of times and when drunk, and I regret the fact that there are now people walking around saying to anyone who will listen, 'I went up to that Richard Webb in the bar afterwards and told him his American accent was rubbish and he had the gall to say that he didn't CARE about my OPINION!' Well, no, I really didn't care because you were being a git. But sensible actors (me! Most of the time! Honest! Don't hate me! Love me! Love me!) will just grin and bear it.

If you can't quite bring yourself or don't trust yourself to tell a bare-faced lie about your friend's performance, then you can always fall back on the old 'hearty double-meaning' strategy. Other actors are especially good at this. They know that their friend and fellow actor has just ballsed it up. They greet them from the other end of the bar with a booming, 'BASTAAARD! YOU'VE DONE IT AGAIN! DRINK!!??' Other stand-bys of this kind include, 'What you did up there really amazed me! Drink?' or 'I've never seen anything quite like that! Drink?' To be honest, this is quite easy to see through, so lying is best.

Of course you could just tell your friend exactly how bad they were. You will probably find this irresistible if you value your own honesty above other people's feelings, i.e. you were brought up on the planet Vulcan or near Liverpool.

3 **Don't be put off by 'luvvie-ness'.** Not many actors of my generation or younger call each other 'luv' or 'luvvie' any more, which I can't help thinking is a pity. But compared to, say, advertising account managers, actors certainly are unusually tactile and kissey. This is partly because they have to form extremely close working relationships at lightning speed. You might have just met an actress two hours ago at the first read-through of a play and now you're simulating sex with her, pretending to punch her in the face or weeping together over the death of your smackhead uncle. Making a big fuss about how friendly and supportive they are to each other is a way for actors to acknowledge that what they do for a living is fucking weird.

So there we have it – know them by their average intelligence, their look of terror and their propensity for kissing. Oh and finally, if you spot a famous one and you want to ask for an autograph, then, well . . . he might have a cold or need a wee or be in a hurry but . . . ask anyway. They love it.

Diary of David Mitchell's Stalker

MONDAY
4

TUESDAY
5

found these pictures of him on the internet.
I reckon if I cut out the right bits of them
I could stick them round the head of an action man
to get a 3D replica. Then I could do anything!

WEDNESDAY
6

Waited outside BBC Television Centre for nine hours hoping
he'd come in for a meeting. I feel it's important to follow up
on that time he nearly looked at me on the tube.

THURSDAY
7   A twelve hour wait today.

Doesn't he do any work?

Doesn't he care!?

RIDAY

Have built a small fluorescent orange tent outside TV centre. It looks like something that gets set up for roadworks but it's not - it's a super-neat home!

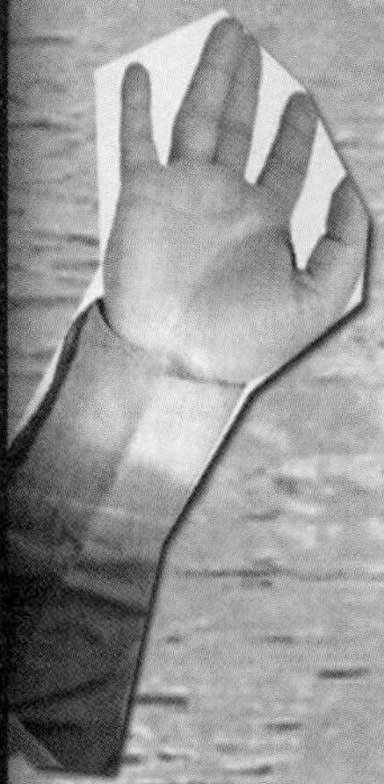

ATURDAY

Kept awake all last night by people queuing to get in to see the One Show. Have decided I hate humans. David would understand.

UNDAY

Managed to sneak into the building with the 'It's a Question of Sport' audience. Then got lost in the corridors and accidentally ended up pitching a couple of shows to BBC Three - they said they're really interested actually.

OTES

David Mitchell
David Mitchell x x
D Mitchell   B. Mitchell
D Mitchell

MAY						
M	T	W	T	F	S	S
18 27	28	29	30	1	2	**3**
19 4	5	6	7	8	9	**10**
20 11	12	13	14	15	16	**17**
18	19	20	21	22	23	**24**
22 25	26	27	28	29	30	31

WEEK 20   MAY

MONDAY
11

Spotted David today! He looked terrific as he strode
towards the building in his jacket and other clothes.
I shouted 'Hi!' as loudly as I could and he looked
startled. Then he said "Oh hi!" am on fire!

TUESDAY
12

Knew when to expect David outside the BBC today
and, sure enough, there he was! This time he stopped
to say hello. I didn't know what to say but he talked
all about the weather - he is amazing!

WEDNESDAY 6am: Spent all last night having imaginary conversations
13   about the weather with my 3D David Mitchell action man doll.
They were a bit samey actually which annoyed me to the point
that I pulled the doll's head off. Whoops! Anyway, am in good practice
for a long weather based chat with David. Can't wait!
2pm: David arrived at BBC at 10am and have only just got away! I mentioned
that it had been raining and that set him off talking about lots of different
sorts of rain, and why they annoy him in different ways, which was fascinating
although did go on for quite a long time. He's got quite a weird voice that
is of course lovely but also gets into my head a bit in a way I'd say I hated
if that wasn't impossible. He's asked for my phone number. Bit weird.

THURSDAY   Spent most of the night fielding David's texts about
14   the weather, and also now cab drivers' attitude to
traffic. His point is that taxi drivers get very irritated by heavy
traffic at busy times when in fact they should expect it. This is of
course an excellent point which is presumably why David chose to make it
to me nine times in nine slightly differently phrased texts. I must say it
was all a bit much, but then I suppose that's what comes of being close
to a star - you burn easily.

RIDAY

5

long weather chat as usual. He's made me promise to sign
up for his podcasts.

ATURDAY

6 Couldn't face waiting outside BBC today so went for a walk
into town. But at 10am on the dot DM was ringing me: "Where
are you? Have you noticed that there's a cold front coming in?
What do you think of my podcasts? You can still get all the
previous ones on iTunes." He is definitely still amazing but also
I did pretend that I was getting bad reception and hung up.

UNDAY

7 ☾

It's foggy today.

Daren't turn my phone on.

NOTES

D.M. D.M. DM

DM. d.m.

d.m.

	MAY						
	M	T	W	T	F	S	S
18	27	28	29	30	1	2	3
19	4	5	6	7	8	9	10
20	11	12	13	14	15	16	17
21	18	19	20	21	22	23	24
22	25	26	27	28	29	30	31

WEEK 21   MAY

MONDAY

18 He's e-mailed me a link to his podcasts. I had a look.
There are hundreds of them in two categories,
'The Weather' and 'Taxi Drivers' attitudes'. I can't
wait to watch them all, although at the same time,
I seem to be able to.

TUESDAY   Had to do some shopping this morning and got back to
19   my little orange tent to discover David already there, making
himself a cup of tea and telling me that Earl Grey was vulgar. He'd eaten
all the Hobnobs but that didn't keep him from forensically analysing what
was wrong with them. I was so overcome to meet my hero in my own home
that for some reason I told him to fuck off. Fortunately he took this
as a joke and stayed for three hours.

WEDNESDAY

20 Have decided to move back to my flat and have taken down the
orange shack. I shall miss it but it did rather smell of DM's mildewy
jacket in the end. He explained that it had got wet a few weeks ago and
never quite dried out because of a humidity problem he's got in his flat.
He explained that in detail. I completely understand exactly how that came
about. I am fully informed to that. Still stinks though.

THURSDAY
21

Roadworks in my street again!

_ A _ I _ M I _ _ _ _ L L

2009

FRIDAY

22 Was walking past the roadworks' fluorescent orange tent, full of nostalgic thoughts for my own former roadside home, then I caught a familiar stench and then even more familiar duck-like nasal prattle. It was David, talking on the phone to his agent about why he thinks 'Argumental' has a flawed format. He really got his point across and I didn't want to disturb him, or for some reason see or speak to him, so I crept gently away.

SATURDAY

23

SUND

24

NOTES

F	S	S
1	2	3
8	9	10
15	16	17
22	23	24
22 25 26 27 28	29 30	31

How to Cope with Servants

David Mitchell

This bit is not really about servants. Even I am not so out of touch that I'd write a section full of comic grievances with domestic staff. Issues such as 'What to do if you think your butler is helping himself to the sherry' and 'Your son has got a housemaid in the family way – how can she discreetly be killed?' are not going to be resolved here.

No one has servants any more. And by 'no one' I don't include me.

That may be unclear. What I mean is: everyone doesn't have servants any more. And by 'everyone' I include me.

Is that any better? I'll try again: I don't have any servants.

I'm not complaining. I think that's fine. I have a washing machine and a hoover – basically, robot servants. I'm living the full 1950s futuristic dream with my mod cons. Except for the flying car. But then again, I don't have a normal car, so I'm perfectly at liberty to imagine that the car that I don't have can fly, thereby making it much more futuristic than all the earthbound cars that other people mistakenly do have.

But the British history of domestic service casts a long shadow. We're basically all massively fucked-up about service-orientated jobs: both doing them and having them done for us. This is because of our deeply ingrained, although to be fair these days more fluid class system.

Can fluids be deeply ingrained? Of course they can! Just look at a coastline or an alcoholic.

The standard British attitude to someone working in a service industry, say a waiter, is one of guilt, shame and consequent hostility.

We assume that a waiter must hate his job and be trying to leave it. It's all right if it's a student or an Australian who we imagine has other priorities and a future, and is only waiting tables in order to earn bungee-jumping money or to pay off an educative loan. But onto any normal waiter we project resentment.

Whatever their manner, we infer they must be screaming inside: 'Why can't little Lord Fauntleroy fetch his own fucking food instead of requiring me, in this day and age, to fetch and carry for him! To bring him exactly what dinner he has ordered from a list of several different dinners, all of which have been brought to a state of near-readiness in an attempt to pre-empt his whim!'

It doesn't occur to us that waiters might take pride in, or even enjoy, their jobs; that they might go to restaurants themselves and be as used to being served food as serving it; that they might see their job as facilitating an activity that everyone takes pleasure in. No, we still see them as domestic servants seething with revolutionary fervour and only kept civil, and in rare cases charming, by their insatiable desire for a tip. But, if we give them a tip, we're sure that that moment of paternalistic largesse is the point at which the waiter will feel most angry and humiliated. In short, we assume bad will and consider it justified.

One of the reasons for this is that, so often, when we Britons work in service-orientated jobs, we genuinely have attitudes not much less resentful than what I've just described. We do find it demeaning. We assume that performing such tasks is to be a mug, is to be the most despised victim of an inegalitarian system. Not that we lift a finger to remove such inequalities – we just deliver people's coffees and sandwiches with a sneer, while British customers smile at us with self-loathing gratitude, forgetting that they are not, in fact, dukes and have never knowingly had a poacher shot. ⟫→

Can fluids be deeply ingrained? Of course they can! Just look at a coastline or an alcoholic.

The attitude in America is quite different. Waiters there are all over you in their keenness to help and improve your dining experience. Yes, they want tips, but they're completely open about that and so dispensing them is a much less embarrassing experience – in no way laced with the feeling of 'throwing a Christmas party for the local children'. Talking to American waiters in a normal way is something even British people can manage. You genuinely feel they don't hate you – the pall of domestic service is not hanging over the interaction.

People doing shit jobs in America can look you in the eye because they believe in their equality, in their ability to become presidents or film stars, despite the overwhelming statistical evidence to the contrary.

This is great for a holiday but ultimately it reveals a society even more delusional than our own. We live in the past: we cling onto old notions of class divisions, either because they reinforce our sense of poshness, reinforce our sense of working-class authenticity or reinforce our sitcom plots. But at least we acknowledge divisions – we more than acknowledge them, we exaggerate them. Despite over sixty years of redistributive taxation, we know we live in a land of haves and have-nots and, even if we're not going to do anything about it, we are aware of it.

But the poor Americans actually think that they're living in a meritocracy – a land of equal opportunity where anyone can be president. This is why so many of them liked George W. Bush – he seemed proof that anyone, even such a prat, could rise to the highest office. They used his incompetence as proof of their utopian society, rather than his multimillionaire heritage as disproof.

People doing shit jobs in America can look you in the eye because they believe in their equality, in their ability to become presidents or film stars, despite the overwhelming statistical evidence to the contrary. And the result of this faith in an omnipotent meritocracy is heartbreaking: it means if they fail, they will only blame themselves. We British, we Europeans, know better. Whatever the complicated truth, we allow ourselves, when we fail, to blame the system.

So, as usual, I've worked my way round to celebrating an element of our fucked-up national psyche that I began by bemoaning. And to think people call me a 'glass-half-empty' type.

But the only way to cope with servants, and service, is to feel no guilt. Television shows have servants; they're called runners and they are often, with a clear conscience, treated like absolute shit. How are British people able to do this? The answer is simply that there is no class division getting in the way and generating guilt. Runners are of the same class – the middle class – as everyone else who works in TV. They're treated badly because many of the people they work for were runners once and were treated badly then. The concepts of 'cycles of abuse' and 'working your way up' perfectly align to get runners screamed at for the slightest error in coffee fetching.

People also feel justified in treating runners badly because of the risk involved, not of revolution – the runners will never rise up – but of a particular runner one day becoming a channel controller. This happens a lot more often than waiters becoming presidents and suits the British sense of sod's law: 'Typical, the runner I threw a baguette at ended up head of BBC One!' This shows that, even when the British do see signs of meritocracy at work, they resent is as much as any other system. I basically love that.

❖

In this painfully, sometimes unreadably frank memoir, snooker commentator and some-time snooker player Peter DeCoursey shares recollections of his life both within and then without the world of professional snooker, in a manner which is both heartbreaking and not suitable for children.

'I've spent my whole life lying on my front, eyeing up balls. Anyway – back to the snooker!'

This is a compelling account of the heady milieu of the snooker scene in the 1970s and '80s, detailing Peter's ongoing battles with convention, alcohol and friend Ted Wilkes.

'Ted walked up and twatted me in the face with an ashtray. "So you're a queer", he said, "Fine. But so help me God, if I ever catch you looking at my arse I will personally beat you to fucking death". I knew then that our friendship was as strong as ever.'

This is a book that will make you laugh, cry, and scrunch your face up like you've just bitten some tin foil.

'It's time to set the record straight. I have never made love on a snooker table. For one thing, like an anus, the baize is a taut and fragile thing. Unlike an anus, you'd be mad to lube it because it's hell to shift. Once you've got lube on the baize, that's it – game over. I learnt that lesson the hard way.'

PRAISE FOR PETER'S PREVIOUS WORK, THE BIG CUSHY PUZZLE BOOK:

'It is an interesting book. It is a book which I have read. It is an interesting book which I have read.'
JOHN MAJOR

'Whaaaar-suh-ffhwaoaaer-yeeeeaaahhhbaaaaarrr!!!'
ALEX HIGGINS

PETER DeCOURSEY

IT STARTED WITH A KISS

SEX, SNOOKER AND ME

St Death in the Vale's Parish Council

Minutes of the last meeting - 26/4/2009

1. Body found in pond.

The discovery of a body floating in the village pond was tearfully lamented by all, and the mood was movingly summed up by the vicar who said of the incident: "Why? Why!? Why!!!??? What's the point in anything!?" The body was discovered to be that of Tim Evans and the consensus was that it wasn't actually suicide so much as "a slow petering out of the will to live – you know, like we all get but worse. Slightly worse."

A minute's silence was then observed to give people the opportunity to self-harm.

2. New parking provisions behind general store.

The vicar opened the discussion with the words: "Who cares, who in the name of fucking Jesus actually cares about any of this shit!?" The motion was carried nem. con.

3. Film night. As usual the choice was between Leaving Las Vegas and Schindler's List. Nobody cared.

Tablet break.

4. Any Other Business: Everyone loves everyone!

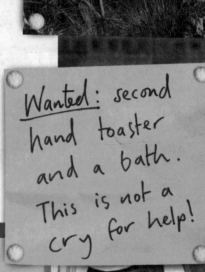

For Sale:

A huge pile of shit that I don't need any more. It's just stuff, you know, and at the end of the day it's meaningless. She's gone. I drove her away. She's never coming back.

<u>Contact:</u> Mr Geoff Edwards — at any hour. I don't sleep. It's like I never will.

Wanted: second hand toaster and a bath. This is not a cry for help!

SAMARITANS

Desperately looking for more volunteers after our branch manager and his wife very sadly took their own lives. We're absolutely rushed off our feet which is incredibly depressing but also kind of takes your mind off things. And when the shift's over, we all hit the sauce and hard!

Take up golf! I've got a hardly used set of left-handed clubs. Used to belong to my wife but now she's in a coma because of pills! You've got to laugh! Life goes on! Even hers nominally!

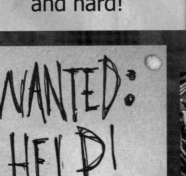

WANTED: HELP!

Self Help Group Announcements

1. The self-help group will be disbanding. It couldn't help itself.
2. Anyone needing self-help should consequently help themselves.
3. Four office chairs available. Help yourselves.

Remembrance Day Service

This year's Remembrance Day Service is cancelled due to last year's three weeks of uncontrollable group sobbing.

BELT AND TIE AMNESTY — THIS FRIDAY!
Put them beyond temptation. Otherwise, as the vicar says, "you're two bottles of whisky to the bad, with a sturdy light-fitting swinging alluringly over your head — what are you going to do? Watch another hour of Quizcall!?"

How to Cope with Getting Older

Robert Webb

❖

I was about 14 when I started buying comedy books and if that's how old you are now, you might be appalled to learn that I haven't had to sit an exam since the year you were born. Believe me, if you're appalled, I'm fucking horrified. I got married when you were 11; the first series of *Peep Show* was made when you were 7; I briefly claimed the Jobseeker's Allowance when you were 1 and I'd finished my GCSEs, passed my driving test and lost my virginity several years before you were born. If this sounds like I'm showing off, I'm really, really not. This is more like dewy-eyed whimsy, something that only old people indulge in.

I'm incredibly old, you see. When I was your age I didn't believe that I could ever be someone who uses the phrase, 'when I was your age'. That was the sort of thing you only heard from people who were nearly dead or seemed better off dead. And it usually preceded some comparison that made the older person sound hard-working and adventurous and the younger person sound unhealthy, lazy, feckless, boring, etc., etc. You never heard: 'When I was your age, I was much more of a stupid wanker than kids seem to be today.' No, it was always: 'When I was your age, I spent the whole time out in the fresh air playing football and snogging girls instead of playing computer games.' I'd have to nod politely while thinking, 'That's because when you were my age, computers hadn't been invented, you pompous old cunt. If you'd been found playing *Jetpack* on a 48K ZX Spectrum in 1951, they'd have burnt you as a witch.'

Technology in general is a fertile area for the old and young to get snooty with each other. When I was at school, there was no Internet, no emails and no mobile phones. And yet somehow – and I know this will impress you – I've managed NOT to draw the conclusion that we were therefore healthier, more fully rounded and generally better children than those of today. I suppose I would also ask younger readers to cut me some reciprocal slack here. Just because we didn't have Facebook didn't make us a bunch of sad-hats with no social life. Is this a plea for tolerance? Oh God, I'm writing A Plea for Tolerance – I must be getting old.

Getting older also means having to cope with your parents getting older. Sadly, my mum died when I was 17 and this was a bit of a downer all round, but one of the upsides is that I don't have to go through the process of watching her going all spazzy with age and senility. No one is going to call me in the middle of the night saying, 'Mum's had another fall/has trapped her foot in the toaster/is marrying a Serbian war criminal', etc. Of course, some people are worth having to cope with, but I seem to have got out of this one scot-free, apart from the heartbreak and terror of abandonment.

Here are some more signs of ageing, along with when they kick in and how to cope:

> **"**
>
> *If you'd been found playing* Jetpack *on a 48K ZX Spectrum in 1951, they'd have burnt you as a witch.*
>
> **"**

Sign
You start making a net loss on Christmas.

When
Late teens

How to Cope
When you realize that you're spending more on Christmas than you're getting back in presents, there are various options. If you're a student and therefore skint, people will basically understand if you just get them all a bag of oranges. Sadly, this won't wash with much younger siblings, nephews, nieces, etc. who have been encouraged to go NUTS at Christmas and will basically want some kind of horse at the very least. Try sending them a card with their name spelt wrong and then ignoring them for five years. This may sound harsh but it will definitely teach them a thing or two about something or other. Otherwise, just take it like the man/woman that you are and tell yourself that Christmas is more about giving than receiving and make sure you buy yourself all the stuff that the other idiots won't think of.

Try sending them a card with their name spelt wrong and then ignoring them for five years.

Sign
You'd rather drink cider than Coke.

When
Fifteen

How to Cope
Don't worry – this won't last. You'll soon be moving on to lager and gin. For the moment, though, it will have to be cider because it's the alcoholic drink that most approximates to a bag of sweeties. Let's face it, that's what most of us would prefer; if I could develop a manly weakness for pear-drops I'd be there like a shot. But society says no.

Sign
You don't really care any more about bad reviews.

When
First BAFTA onwards

How to Cope
This may not be completely universal but I feel the need to share. If you're worried that you've become too mature, well disciplined and emotionally secure to care what critics think of you, try reading a bad review in the morning, leave to simmer all day, go to the pub and have a row with your ex-girlfriend, come home angry and drunk, read the review again and then attend to your Twitter account. You'll be back to your aggressively self-righteous twenty-something self in no time!

Sign
You start going bald.

When
Twenty-seven

How to Cope
Again, this only really applies to men and only to those men who start going bald when they're 27. Many women will tell you that they couldn't care less that you're going bald and I find that a key strategy is to believe them. Another good idea is to avoid going into a profession that puts a high premium on conventional ideas of physical attractiveness. Such as acting. Oh dear.

"Now that's what I call
an egg sandwich."

T.S. ELIOT

KINGDOM of HEAVEN

WHO'S BETTER,
JESUS OR MOHAMMAD?
THERE'S ONLY ONE WAY TO FIND OUT!

"A sensitive handling of the historical causes of perhaps our most dinner-party ruining foreign policy dilemma." **heat**

great flat-share fridge note discourses 4:

peter mandelson and keith harris

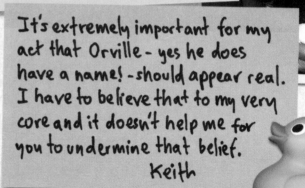

Keith — Scattering feathers in the fridge is never going to make me think that it's your fucking duck that's finished the margarine rather than you!
Peter

It's extremely important for my act that Orville — yes he does have a name! — should appear real. I have to believe that to my very core and it doesn't help me for you to undermine that belief.
Keith

Does the same thing go for the fucking monkey? I basically can't bring bananas into the house!?
Peter

It's all one-way isn't it!? I'm charm personified to your weird friend Tony when he sleeps on the sofa and makes the lounge smell of feet and yet you're allowed to be racist to Cuddles.
Keith

It's not racist to call Cuddles a monkey! He is, by your own admission and at most, a monkey! What's racist is your equating calling a monkey a monkey with racism!
Peter

Look, I like a joke as much as anyone but can I say that Orville is actually rather an expensive piece of stage equipment and aralditing your moustache hair to his beak is not funny. Keith

vote
Labour

You also called him a cunt.
Keith

If he could fly like a real duck, he wouldn't have let me.
Peter

He is a cunt. We need to have a house meeting.
Peter

Don't you understand. HE WISHES HE COULD FLY RIGHT UP TO THE SKY BUT HE CAN'T!!.
Keith

TORY
BOY

Peter – Please don't be upset. The meeting got a bit heated as you know and when I said your moustache looked 'gay' I meant it in the modern slang sense of 'naff' rather than homosexual. Not that I'd have a problem either way. Keith

He can't? Peter

He can't.
Keith

It's too late to backtrack now. I'm shaving it off!
Peter

When will you get the message, Keith, that I HATE THAT DUCK!!!
Peter

REJECTED POSTER DESIGNS FOR GREAT MOVIES No. 11

EQUUS
Everyone has to draw a line.
His is nosey horses.

Our new music critic, Clive View, steels himself for the greatest ordeal of his career, reviewing James Blunt in concert!

I thought I was lucky to have this job. To be paid to appreciate the work of some of the greatest musicians in the world – to be in a position to promote and celebrate talent.

And then my editor told me that on Friday night, I was going to have to go and watch the biggest dick in the world piss and jizz and, by anatomical miracle, shit on a room full of hatefully grateful paying customers. If there's a lower form of life than James Blunt it can only be the teeming millions of his verminous fans.

And so I stood among them as the sainted prick turd stepped onto the stage holding his fucking guitar and started to play one of his songs all of which are, as anyone will tell you, absolutely awful and inexcusable and literally worse than listening to a cat being strangled. I mean, really everyone says that so it must be true.

But everyone around me seemed to be really enjoying them – it was like being at a Nuremberg rally (although admittedly more concerty and with infinitely fewer genocidal opinions being expressed)! But basically he is Hitler. James Blunt is Hitler as any proper music lover will tell you. And his painful death

"The consensus is that he's a massive nobhead"

would be a good thing, even for him – that's what my friend Andrew said in the pub and it felt incredibly funny and true, like a sitcom based on class differences.

So, anyway, death to the fascist guitar-hugging arsehead, I inwardly screamed while slightly listening to the music which is so bad it gives a deceitful impression of being at least okay. That's how evil it is! It's not really good, it just pretends, like methodone or oven chips or Jacob's Creek.

"How long until the end?" I asked someone in desperation. "About one minute," they said so that was okay to be fair. But, honestly, what a fucking evil bastard witch cock Hitler with his bloody guitar songs and his fans!?

I mean, I totally understand that he is terrible – but it's difficult to describe why. His music is sort of fine-sounding – but it isn't really fine, of course, I'm not saying that for a moment, it's awful. It just briefly sounds okay or a bit

good so fools listen to it or buy it when they'd be better off doing other things – they could be mature students, for example. There's no way that the arsehole Blunt is helping the Open University at all with his songs that any idiot could tell could be bettered. And why doesn't he better them? Either evilness or ineptitude – or, worse, both.

So don't go to any of his other concerts, I'd say. It's academic anyway, as they're all sold out – to twats! But sold out, nevertheless.

He used to be in the army – what's that about?

So, anyway, if excellence in music is what you're looking for then you probably know where to find it anyway. If not, listening to James Blunt will not help you – there's a risk you'll think he's okay which is incredibly socially costly. So take my advice and hate him and be horrible about him in conversations – that always goes down well. And it's easy to forget that he's a person.

Although I do feel a bit bad. I mean, he can play the guitar and everything. I didn't even stick at the recorder. And, as I type this, I know there are features in Microsoft Word that I'm not getting the benefit of.

Obviously I also know that Microsoft Word is awful and useless – just in a slightly useful way that everyone uses.

Rex Features

Further Reading

There isn't really room for a full bibliography, but if you enjoyed *This Mitchell and Webb Book*, here are some of the more obvious publications that you might want to read.

Alexeev, N.P. 2004. *On Danger of Clothes and Benefits of Nudity*

Altenberg, Bengt. 1987. *Causal Ordering Strategies in English Conversation.* J. Monaghan, ed., *Grammar in the Construction of Texts*, 50–64. London: Frances Pinter.

Ashby, William J. 1988. *The Syntax, Pragmatics, and Sociolinguistics of Left- and Right-Dislocations in French. Lingua* 76:203-229.

Barnsley, Michael F., and Stephen G. Demko., ed. 1986. *Chaotic Dynamics and Fractals.* San Diego, CA: Academic Press, Inc.

Barth-Weingarten, Dagmar and Elizabeth Couper-Kuhlen. 2002. *On the Development of Final Thought: a Case of Grammaticalization?*

Carley, Caroline. 1981. *Inventory of Cultural Resources in the Chilkoot and White Pass Units of Klondike Gold Rush National Historical Park. Reconnaissance Report* 40. Office of Public Archaeology, University of Washington, Seattle

Chang, Chung-yin. 1997. *A Discourse Analysis of Questions in Mandarin Conversation.* National Taiwan University MA thesis.

Clayton, D.D., 1983, *Principles of Stellar Evolution and Nucleosynthesis* (Chicago: Univ. of Chicago Press).

Couper-Kuhlen, Elizabeth and Tsuyoshi Ono, eds. 2007. *Turn Continuation in Cross-linguistic Perspective. Pragmatics* 17.4.

Dose, K., and Zaki, L., 1971, *The Peroxidatic and Catalytic Activity of Hemoprotenoids. Z. Naturforsch*

Drew, Paul and Elizabeth Holt. 1988. *Complainable Matters: The Use of Idiomatic Expressions in Making Complaints.* Social problems 35.4: 398-417.

Haines Service and Repair Manual 100 Saloon and Estate (Avant), Oct 82 – 90, up to H, 1.8 litre (1781cc), 1.9 litre (1921cc), 2.0 litre (1994cc), 2.1 litre (2144cc), 2.2 litre (2226cc) and 2.3 litre (2309cc) Does NOT cover Quattro or Diesel

Hasselhoff, David, 2007, *Don't Hassel the Hoff! The Autobiography.* Thomas Dunne Books

Holmes, C.E. 1990 *The Broken Mammoth Site: Its Relevance in Alaska/Yukon Prehistory.* Paper presented at the annual meeting of the Canadian Archaeological Association, Whitehorse, Yukon Territory

Hudson, Robert. 2009. *The Kilburn Social Club.* Jonathan Cape

Leffler, S., McKusick M., Karels, M. and Quarterman, J. 1990. *The Design and Implementation of the 4.3 BSD Unix Operating System.* Addison-Wesley

Li, F., Bartz, D., Gu, L, Audette, M.A., *An Iterative Classification Method of 2D CT Head Data based on Statistical and Spatial Information*

Louv, Richard. 2006. *Last Child in the Woods: Saving Our Children from Nature-Deficit Disorder.* Algonquin Book

Mishkenot Sha'ananim Newsletter 7. December 1986. *Deconstruction. A Trialogue with Geoffrey Hartman and Wolfgang Iser.* Jerusalem

Sutton, G.P. *Rocket Propulsion Elements: An Introduction to the Engineering of Rockets* (6th ed. 1992)

Price, Alfred. 2005. *The Rocket Firing Typhoons in Normandy: Two Major Actions. Air Power Review,* 8:1, 79–88. Publisher: RAF Magazines. ISSN 1463-6298.

Price, Katie, 2009. *Jordan: Pushed to the Limit.* Arrow

Pagel, B.E.J., 1987, in *A Unified View of the Macro and Micro Cosmos,* ed. A. De Rujula, D.V. Nanopoulos, and P.A. Shaver, (World Scientific: Singapore)

Mengel, J.G., and A.V. Sweigart, 1981, *Astrophysical Parameters for Globular Clusters,* edited by A.G.D. Philip (Reidel, Dordrecht)

Toxen, Bob, 2003, *Real World Linux Security: Intrusion Prevention, Detection, and Recovery,* 2nd edition, Prentice-Hall

Wm. Ray Heitzmann. 2006. *Opportunities in Marine Science and Maritime Careers,* revised edition, McGraw-Hill

Index

A

A Year in Provence (Mayle) 44
Abba 70, 146
Abbott, Russ 109
Abha Gold (cheese) 83
Academic Action Team (AAT)
 152
Ackbar, Admiral: co-designs 'B-
 wing' starfighter 117, 119; feud
 with Mon Mothma 154, 157,
 159–163; indigestion during
 Battle of Endor 432
actors, How to Cope With 227–9
Allen Key, Mitchell and Webb 69
Allen, Damien 14, 15
Allen, Tristram 14, 15
Altitude 119–27
Amis, Martin 16–17
Amsterdam (McEwan) 142
Andre, Peter 109
anti-drugs advertisements, DM
 and RW in one of their 93
Applause from the Other Table
 (Wilkes) 206–7
Apple Computers 213
Ash, Timothy Garton 33
Association of West End Theatres
 185
Atta, Mohammed 130
Atlantis, holidays in 19
At Time of Writing (Hare) 205
Ayckbourn, Alan: *Absurd Person
 Singular* destroys Heath
 government 143; 'ethics in golf'
 campaign 276; Lord Protector
 of Scarborough 187, 189;
 Princess Margaret 'front-fasten'
 scandal 148–152

B

BAFTA 247
Balkans 104
Banqueting House, DM's rallying
 cry for Protectionism fails to
 impress the guests at the 98
Barby, David 57
Bargain Hunt 56, 57, 145, 146
Basic Instinct 51
Baskervillior-Zapp, Aspiratiana 56
Bassey, Shirley 44
Batter Sea Power Station 200
Bazalgette, Joseph: sewage 221
Bazalgette, Peter: sewage 12, 35,
 76, 143
BBC 22, 230, 232, 234, 239; BBC1
 on a Saturday Night 28;
 Broadcast Dash It All! Form
 183; Broadcast Fuck Form 22;
 champagne and swearing
 evening 213; DM and RW at a
 planning meeting 96; 'Salt of
 the Sitcom' campaign 11;
 The One Show 176
Beach, The 29
Beckett, Samuel 16
being dumped, How to Cope
 With, part one: denial and
 despair 36–9; How to Cope
 With, part two: revenge and
 renewal 162–5
Belgravia Security Associates 9
Bellow, Saul 17
Bendicks 184
Bennett, Alan 54
Berlin Wall 104
Big Ben 202
Big Red Amphibious Vehicle
 Guide to London, The 199–202
Bin Laden, Osama: failed
 Eurovision bid 432; gay icon 35,
 38; turns down 'dictionary
 corner' on *Countdown* 443
Blabton IX, King 44
Black, Cilla: 'inexplicable
 popularity' 206; snubbed by
 UKIP 239, 241
Blair, Cherie 184
Blair, Tony 222; Cabinet, RW at
 first picture of 108; Michael
 Sheen as 186; séance and
 lawnmower party 184
Blessed, Brian 222
Blumenthal, Heston 104
Blunt, James 253
Blur 32
'Bognor Regis is full of plebs'
 (RW's report for the *Holiday*
 programme) 96
Buck Rogers in the 25th Century 88
Bond, James: fridge-note
 discourse with Darth Vader 4, 5;
 murder of Diana, Princess of
 Wales 202
Bono 103
Booker Prize 142
Boots 113
Bowles, Peter 99
Brand, Russell 109
Brandreth, Gyles: recipe for
 perfect Pimm's 232; inventor of
 hovercraft 123; teddy-bear
 obsession 12
British Army 185
British National Party 3
Broccoli, Cubby 101
Buckingham Palace 101, 202
Bullitt 20
BUPA 194
Bush, George W. 238

C

Cable, Vince 213
Cadbury 178
Cambridge Footlights 94
Cameron, David 33
CAMRA 29
Carr, Jimmy: bogeys, bacteria
 build-up causes 131; as Dignity
 in *Death with Dignity* 73;
 dreams 131; piss stains on
 trousers and underwear 131;
 shoes, cleanliness of 131
Carthage, holidays in 18
Caruso, David, 156–7
Cash, Craig 44

Castle, Roy 208

Casualty 28

Chamberlain, Neville 152, 153

Channel 4 222

Chaplin 154

Charlemagne 226

Charles II, King 201

Charles, Ray 103

Cheddah (cheese) 83

Cheese Week 206

Cheese World 206

Chelsea Physic Garden 200

Churchill, Winston 152, 153, 206

'Cinema in the Buff' 192

Circle of Shame 128–31

Civilization IV (computer game) 88

Clarkson, Jeremy 18, 206

Clooney, George 128

Club 18–30 206

Cobain, Kurt: meadows 65; Tango campaign 145–146, 198; Ulster talks 190–197

Coe, Seb 44

coffee, How to Cope With 78–81

Comic Relief 196–7

Confetti 106, 192

Consignia – the Making of a Mistake (Morgan) 186

Coronation Street 33

Count the Dots 188

Creative Writing Tips 141; week one: the short story 142–4; sample short story 145–6

Crowe, Russell 156

Crying Game, The 100

CSI Miami 156, 158

Culshaw, John 186

Current Emergency, money saving tips for the 132–3; module 1 – staying warm 132; module 2 – eating 133; module 3 – morale 133; module 4 – travel 133

Cybermen, The: destruction of home planet 12–14; destruction of Cyber Fleet 15; failure to convert Earth into New Mondas 19, failure to defeat The Doctor 12–19, 24–28, 35–41, 43, 49, 58, 62, 74, 89–94, 100–106, 108, 124, 127–163, 168, 170, 172–174, 180–183, 201, 208–212; failure to destroy Voga, Planet of Gold 24, 26; slaughtered by Daleks 26–28; slaughtered by Raston Warrior Robot 35–36, Time War irrelevance 43; vulnerability to EMP devices 49, 58, 62; vulnerability to gold 74, 89–94, 100–106; vulnerability to heavy explosives 124, 127–163; vulnerability to solvents 168, 170, 172–174; vulnerability to radiation 180–183, 201, 208–212

D

Daily Mail 26

Damned United, The (Morgan) 186, 222

Daniels, Paul 16–17

'David Frost interviews Tony Blair on Frost on Sunday' 186

David Starkey's Complete History of England 46–7

de Klerk, F.W. 104

Dead Ringers 186

Death with Dignity 73

DeCoursey, Peter: age of 127; AIDS and 122; 'I Love Snooker and Am Gay' *Altitude* article 119–27; *It Started with a Kiss: Sex Snooker and Me* 240–1; Ted Wilkes and 120, 240

Del Monte, the man from 29

Diana, Princess of Wales 202

diary of David Mitchell's stalker 230–5

Diaz, Cameron 129

Dickinson, David 143

Digby and Ginger's Game of Life and Death 6–7

Discovery channel 99

Disgraceful Things You Can Learn from the Internet: No. 206: How to Set Fire to a Cat 176–7; No. 403: How to Stab the Queen 40–1

Disguises (McEwan) 142

Don't Go Dotty 190

Don't Go Dotty! Oh She's Gone! 190

Don't Take the Love of Vectron into the Bath or You'll Set Fire to the Water! 57

Dots Challenge 189

Dr Who 89

Drago, Tony 113

Driscoll, Brian 161

Driscoll, Kath 161

Driscoll, Mandy 161

E

E.T. The Extra-Terrestrial 43

EastEnders 26, 33

Eco, Umberto 212

Economist, The 92

Edinburgh Fringe 97

Edwards, Geoff 242

Edwards, Huw 61

Egan, Peter 44

Eliot, T. S. 248

Elizabeth II, Queen, how to stab 40–1; Commonwealth Games and 40; disguise, using 40; invincibility of Queen and 41; MBE and 40; on Royal walkabout 40; stabqueen.org 40; what will I need? 40–1; where to stab her, illustration of 41

Elton, Ben 32

Emergency Medical Treatment (Gibson/Turner) 141

Empire Strikes Back, The 57

Equus 252

Eubank, Chris 101

Evans, Tim 242

Eve, Trevor 157

Expert Examinations for Social Induction & Education (eesie) 178

F

Facebook 245

Fare's Fair 134

fears grow for fate of Dorset exchange student in North Korea 198

Ferrari, Nick 192

Ferris, Gorden 11

fish milk 84

'Flashdance' – The Artist at Work 196–7; The Artist in Time 196; The Artist Prostrate 196–7; The Artist as TruthSayer 197; The Artist as Warrior 197; The Artist at Rest 197

flat-share fridge note discourses, great: 1: Darth Vader and James Bond 4–5; 2: Paul Daniels and Martin Amis 16–17; 3: Helen Keller and Danii Minogue 70–1; 4. Peter Mandelson and Keith Harris 250–1

48K ZX Spectrum 245

'Freak Medical Condition', David Mitchell hospitalised with 72

Freedland, Jonathan 33

Freeman, Martin 91

Freemantle Media 184

French Army 185

French, Philip 33

Frost/Nixon (Morgan) 222

Frost, David 186, 222

Fry, Stephen: actor and world class boffin 227; investigation of Bi-Polar Disorder 58; further reading 252–3

G

Galloway, George: admiration for Mao 123–156; admiration for Saddam Hussein 78, 98,129–154; admiration for Stalin 143–256; 12,14, 43,76, 143–152, 234; friendship with Tariq Aziz 230–598; humiliation on Big Brother 54; inevitable disgrace 86

Game of Life and Death, Digby and Ginger's 6–7

Garfunkel's 134

Gascoigne, Paul 19

Gaskell, Elizabeth: attempts to adapt *Cranford* as limerick 85–89, 102; early super-foods advocate 36–38; bicycle-rocketry experiments 43, 45; World's Strongest Man disqualification 62

Gaul and Bladder 134

GCHQ Intercepted Dialogue 76–7

Geller, Ross (PhD.) adopts Capuchin monkey 99; Carol Willick divorce 104; tension over Rachel Green Bloomingdale's decision 321–322

General Certificate of Secondary Education: History 152–3; Mathematics 178–9

getting older, How to Cope With 244–7

Ghazzalah Devotional Wensleydale (cheese) 82

Gibson, John 141–6

Gill, AA: emotional problems 89; friendship with Ross Kemp 176; haemorrhoids 121; obsession with moisturiser 345; penis complaint 39–40; role in Black Death 479, swinging 13, 15, 18–21, 143–149, 200, 203, 267–268

Glastonbury Festival 32

Glee, Mark 23

Goal-Oriented Learning with David Beckham 86–7

Goldfinger, Auric: body-paint enthusiast 74; disputes Keith Waterhouse is inventor of 'the egg trick' 54; Richard Dimbleby Lecture 243

Good/Bad at Art spectrum 2

Goon Show 65

Göring, Hermann 140

Grand Temple of the Holy Eye of the Storm of Vectron's Dreadful Love 56–7

Grantham, Leslie: cab-driver stabbing 254, online fan-wank 255, quiet life 256

Gray, Linda 103

Grayling, A.C. 53

Greenpeace 206

greeting cards, Mitchell and Webb multi-purpose 135–9

Griffin, Nick 3; favourite milkshakes 12; Lego 127–130, 134, 138; 'What I Did In The Holidays' 227

Groundhog Day 64

Guardian 32, 44, 228

Gucci 194

H

Handley, Tommy 65

Hare, David 205

Harris, John 32

Harris, Keith 250–1

Harrods 201

Harry Potter 165

Hastings, Max 32

Havers, Nigel 105

Hawking, Stephen (Prof.) *A Brief History of Time* 243; supporting artist 111–115; Olympics disappointment 302

headline puns, newspaper industry's pre-prepared cache of 60–3

Health Commission adverts 10, 52, 150

Heath, Ted 224

Help the Thick 48–9

Help Yourself with David Caruso 156–9; Tip One: How To Be A Good Actor 157; Tip Two: How To Look Thinner 158; Tip Three: How To Look Fatter 159

Hendry, Stephen 127

Herring, Jemima 84

Hewitt, Patricia 61

Higgins, Alex: comments on *It Started with a Kiss: Sex, Snooker and Me* (DeCoursey) 240; wins at Crucible whilst seeing double 206

Hilton, Paris 109

Himmler, Heinrich 140

History Man, The (Bradbury) 144

Hitler, Adolf 152, 153; madness of 3; speeches of 28; 10 Lost Text Messages 140

Hiya! (magazine) 109–17

Hoffman, Dustin 122

Hogg, Douglas: moat maintenance 209

Holiday 96

holidays in places that don't exist any more: Atlantis 19; Carthage 18; Humberside 19; Troy 19

Hollyoaks 228

Holness, Matthew 101
Hospice, Mitchell and Webb 65
House of Commons 224; DM's maiden speech in 93
How to Cope With: actors 227–9; being dumped part one: denial and despair 36–9; being dumped part two: revenge and renewal 162–5; being normal 1–3; coffee 78–81; getting older 244–7; nudists 192–5; pubs 26–9; servants 236–9; staying in a Malmaison Hotel 28, 180–2; the smoking ban 208–11
How We Met: Margaret Thatcher and Captain Todger 224–5
Humberside, holidays in 19
Hunt, Tristram 33

I

'I Love Snooker And Am Gay' (DeCoursey) 119–27
In the Air Tonight 94
In Vitro We Trust 72
'Intergalactic Fund for the Discovery of Who Vectron Is' 57
Isle of Dogs 202
It Started with a Kiss: Sex Snooker and Me (DeCoursey) 240–1

J

Jackson, Michael: on children 43; on Deification 68; on fire 107
Jenkins, Simon 33
Jetpack 245
Jizan Brie (cheese) 83
Jones, Gryff Rhys 58
Justice for the Just OKs 49

K

Kaufman, Gerald: dislike of prawns 345; Fish Club 23, 47, 34–35, 54–59; preference for halibut 98
Keller, Helen 70–1
Kennedy, Charles 96, 184
Khafjian Pebble Stilton (cheese) 82
Khan, Genghis 31
Kids Just Don't Know Their Woods, Mitchell and Webb's 24–5
Kingdom of Heaven 249
kippers 85
kittieburn.co.uk 176–7
knighthoods, RW and DM receive their 101
Knowles, Eric 56, 57
Kournikova, Anna 100
Kyle, Jeremy: bridge partner of General Pinochet 54; 'worthless chancer' 67–69, 72

L

Lady Patricia Wilberforce's Sex Hour 183
Lakeview Cottage – Visitors Book No. 4 34–5
Landfill, Mitchell and Webb Cheap 147
Lane, Carla 14
Langham, Chris 15
Larkin, Philip 57
Law, Jude 128
Lawson, Luc 93
Lawson, Mark 93
Lazy Writers Guide to Writing 141–6; week one: the short story 142–4; sample short story 145–6
Leaving Las Vegas 242
Leicestershire 193
Levi, Primo 150
Liberal Democrat Fundraiser 184
Littlejohn, Richard 228
London Aquarium 202
London Arms, The 202
London Brain, The 202
London Eye, The 202
London Fashion Week 203
London Legs, The 202
London Paper 53
London Torso, The 202
Lord's Cricket Ground 200
Lost in Translation 64
Lovelock, Toby 198
Lucky People Live Longer – Official 53
Lulu 99
Lusardi, Linda 206
Luton Airport 200

M

Mac vs PC the journey 107, 213–21; Arms Dealers 219; Catholic Church in Africa, The 221; Chewing Gum 216; Cigarettes 217; Nintendo Wii 214; Kellogg's Corp Internal Video 215; Recreational Drugs 218; Sex Industry, The 220
Mack, Lee 90
madness, definition of 1, 2–3
Madagascar, DM in 99
Madonna 184
Major, John 240
Making of Star Stories, The 222
Malcontent, Professor 44
Malmaison Hotel, How to Cope With Staying in a 28, 180–2
Man, Derek 23
Mandelson, Peter 250–1
Marlboro 79
Matrix, The 105
Mayle, Peter 44
Mayo, Simon 227
McEwan, Ian 142
McGee, Debbie 16, 17
McGill, Grand High Bishop Excelsior 57
McKeith, Gillian (Dr): actual academic qualifications 29; claims of odourless shit 71; importance of lying 112; lying 123, 143–148, 230
McKenna, Paul 88, 142
McQueen, Steve 20
Meaning of a Bad Back, David Mitchell and the 58
Mein Kampf 140
MI5, RW recruited by 95
Mighty Boosh, The 166–73
Milan Fashion Show, 1989 102
Milkybar Kids 101
Miller, Dr Jonathan 53
Milne, Seamus 33
Minogue, Danii 70–1
Mirren, Helen 130
Mitchell and Web Clones, The 97
Mock the Week 91
Monbiot, George 32
Money Saving Tips for the

Current Emergency 132–3
Monroe, Marilyn 74
Morgan, Peter 186, 222
Morton, Samantha 94
Mothma, Mon: feud with Admiral Ackbar 154, 157, 159–163; regrets 'Bothan Spies Wanted' classified ad. 155; sued by families of Bothan Spies 158
mundane quotes of the great: No. 1 Genghis Khan 31; No. 2 George Orwell 50; No. 3 Harold Pinter 58; No. 4 Sir Isaac Newton 68; No. 5 Marilyn Monroe 74; No. 6 Primo Levi 150; No. 7 Sting 204; No. 8 Umberto Eco 212; No. 9 Florence Nightingale 223; No. 10 Charlemagne 226; No. 11 T. S. Eliot 248
Mussolini, Benito 140
Mustard Powder Tins, Mitchell and Webb 69
My Shags as a Whore (Gibson/Turner) 141

N

National Polo Players' Awards 101
NATO 225
Nessun Dorma 228
New Labour 55
News of the World, The 225
Newton, Sir Isaac 68
Nightingale, Florence 223
Nixon, Richard 98
normal, How to Cope With being 1–3
North Circular, The 200
Not While I've Got My Strength 72
nudists, How to Cope With 192–5
Number 1, London 201
Nureyev, Rudolf: early life in Lincoln 345, 349–354; lead soloist with Kirov Ballet 378; publication of memoir, *Does My Cock Look Big In This!?* 397

O

O'Sullivan, Ronnie 206
Oasis 32
Obama, Barack 33; *Jim'll Fix It* bitterness 64; lambasts *Jim'll Fix It* rules as 'draconian' 67
Observer Woman 23
One Show, The 176
Orwell, George 50
Outbreak 75
Oxford University Press 93
Oxo Tower 184

P

Palace of Westminster 202
Pants Labyrinth 185
Parish Notices: Ponton-by-the-Wealth 8–9; St Death in the Vale's; 242–3; St Salmon's 84-85; Scuzby-on-Swill 160–1
Parkinson/Castro (Morgan) 186
Parkinson, Michael 57, 186
Pasteur, Ariadne 53
Peep Show 65, 69, 244
Penn's Pens 184
'People with No Legs Do Less Walking' (Plaster) 53
Peter Morgan's New Idea for a Drama: *Consignia – The Making of a Mistake* 186; *The Making of Star Stories* 222
Peters, Andy: Bloody Sunday 36–37, 42, 48; Haiku champion 321, Schleswig-Holstein question 104–107; sinking of Rainbow Warrior 235
pictures, autobiographical 93–108; Ad campaign for tramps' shoes 99; anti-drugs advertisements, DM and RW in one of their 93; 'Bognor Regis is full of plebs' (RW's report for the *Holiday* programme) 96; DM and Anna Kournikova 100 ; DM and RW at BBC planning meeting 96; DM and RW flank Michael Jackson 94; DM in Madagascar 99; DM in *The Crying Game* 100; DM relaxing in the pool with first wife,

Linda Gray 103; DM with Charles Kennedy 96; DM with U2 103; House of Commons, DM's maiden speech in 93; Milkybar kids reunion 101; National Polo Player's Awards with Chris Eubank, DM at 101; Richard Nixon and RW 98; RW and DM receive their knighthoods 101; RW and Lulu 99; RW and MI5 95; RW at Milan Fashion Show, 1989 102; *The Mitchell and Webb Clones* 97; *Up the Bunkum* 94; Verne Troyer, DM, RW and 95; warplane 95; *Whoops Palindrome!* 94
Pike family 85
Pinter, Harold 58, 176
Pizza Express: and sinking of Atlantis 19; debate over quality of 134; number of outlets within London area 202; Venice and 202
Plaster, Kevin 53
Plath, Sylvia 129
Poison, Mitchell and Webb 67
Polythene, Mitchell and Webb 65
Ponton-by-the-Wealth Hunt 9
Prancing in My Dark Heart – The Flashdance Years (Webb) 185
Prescott, John: diving for pearls 67–69; lead soloist with Bolshoi Ballet 235, 237
pubs, How to Cope with 26–9
puzzle, Mitchell and Webb's 187–91; Don't Go Dotty 190; Don't Go Dotty! Oh She's Gone! 190; Dots Challenge 189; Pseudocu! 191

Q

Question Time 228

R

Radio Five Live 227
Rain Man 92
Ramsay, Gordon 23
rantingisfree.com 21
Ray Winstone University,

Norwich 53
Real Deal 143
RedBurp Productions 58
Redgrave, Vanessa 228
rejected poster designs for great movies: No. 1 *Bullitt* 20; No. 2 *Titanic* 30; No. 3 *E.T. The Extra-Terrestrial* 43; No. 4 *Basic Instinct* 51; No. 5 *Lost in Translation* 64; No. 6 *Outbreak* 75; No. 7 *Rain Man* 92; No. 8 *Schindler's List* 149; No. 9 *Chaplin* 154; No. 10 *Kingdom of Heaven* 249; No. 11 *Equus* 252
Regency De Montfort Hair and Tricology Systems Clinic 42
Repossession Solutions, Mitchell and Webb 155
Reservoir Dogs 205
review 66–7
Rhodes, Gary 206
Robert Webb Has More Money Than Sense 73
Rock the Languedoc 103
Rogers, Anton: good in bed 45, 47–49; Oscar nomination for Son of Pink Panther 87; rivalry with Julia McKenzie 89; SAS years 312, 314
Ronaldo, Cristiano: can't swim 232, prefers tennis 321
Roosevelt, Theodore 107
Ross, Jonathan 62
Rowling, J.K. 165
Royal Mail 186
Rutland 193
Ryan, Meg 156

S

Sakakan Gas Cheese 82
Samaritans 243
Sand (cheese) 83
sardines 85
Saudi Arabia, cheeses of 82–3; Abha Gold 83; Cheddah 83; Ghazzalah Devotional Wensleydale 82; Jizan Brie 83; Khafjian Pebble Stilton 82; Sakakan Gas Cheese 82; Sand 83; Smoked Gold 83

Savile, Jimmy 174
Sblabtons 44
Schama, Simon 228
Schindler's List 149, 242
Serrell, Philip 57
servants, How to Cope With 236–9
set fire to a cat, how to 176–7; BBC's *The One Show* and 176; good places to set fire to a cat 176; Harold Pinter on 176; kittieburn.co.uk; 176–7; paraffin 176, 177
Shakespeare, William 175
Sheen, Michael 186, 222
Sherrin, Ned 58
Silk Cut 79
Silver, Andrew 205
sitcom, pitch for a working-class 11–15
Sky 28
Slapeaze™ 42
'Smiling Makes You Look Happy' (Plaster) 53
smoking ban, How to Cope With the 208–11
Smoked Gold (cheese) 83
Snooker Week 206
Snooker World 206
snookerparadise.com 115
Speciousephemera 172–3
speed cameras 55
St Andards 185
St Death in the Vale's Parish Council 242–3
St Paul's Cathedral 201
St Peter's International Relations Discussion Group 8
St Ringfellow, Peter 184
St Salmon's Parish Council 84–5
St Stephen's Tower 202
stabqueen.org 40
Stalin, Joseph 140
Star Wars 78
Starbucks 79
Starkey, David 46–7
Stein, Rick 85
Sting, Sting 204; balloon animal record 276, expulsion from Magic Circle 401–403; Hale and Pace shrine 374

Stockton, Lord 8
Stockton, Lady 8
Stop Going Bald Now! 42
Stranger Than Fiction Publishing 185
Sun, The 75
Sykopath, Jeremy 66

T

Tales of Nemo Magnolia (Zoologist & Tuber Guru) Part 904: The Moon Darkens Brightly Don't They 170–1
Talk Radio 192
Tea Towel, This Mitchell and Webb 82–3
Ten Celebrity Cancer Deaths for Easter (Morgan) 186
Ten Things I Love About Vectron (Larkin) 57
Terry Wogan's Home 202
Thatcher, Margaret: How We Met: Captain Todger and 224–5
The Best Bit… Of the Entire Book… 174
Thorn Birds, The 17
Titanic 30
Todger, Captain 44, 45; How We Met: Margaret Thatcher and 224–5
To-Do List: David's 90–1; Robert's 88–9
Toilet Paper, Mitchell and Webb 148
Took, Barry 61
Top Gear 206
Torode, John 29
Torsa, Island of 9
Tower of London 201
Toynbee, Polly 32
Trading Places 192
tramps' shoes 99
Trotter, Derek: buys Filofax 165; censures brother as 'plonker' 167–175, mawkish references to dead mother 168, 170, 174, 182; reflects on chandelier incident 181
Troy, holidays in 18
Troyer, Verne 95

Turner, Andrew 141–6
Tuscany 132
TV pitches, Robert's failed: *Death with Dignity* 73; *In Vitro We Trust* 72; *Not While I've Got My Strength* 72; *Robert Webb Has More Money Than Sense* 73

U

Up the Bunkum 94
Upright/Easy-Going spectrum 2
U2 103

V

Vader, Darth 4–5
Vectron 56, 57
Vegas, Johnny 73
Venice, Pizza Express and 202
Victims of Untragic Death 49
View, Clive: fashion critic, reviews London Fashion Week 203; music critic, reviews James Blunt 253; restaurant critic, reviews the *Gaul and Bladder*, Wantage 134; theatre critic, reviews *At Time of Writing* by David Hare 205

W

Waitrose 79
Waking the Dead 157
Wallace, Danny 23
Wan, Gok 23, 61
Wantage 134
Waterstone's 1
Westwood, Vivienne 102
What Have You Done with the Vinyl Father? 168–9
What Minibreak? (magazine) 18
Wellington, Duke of 201
whitebait 85
Why Have All The Walls Got Lower? 32–3
Wilkes, Asti 109–17
Wilkes, Kevin 23
Wilkes, Ted: *Applause from the Other Table: My Life in Snooker* 206–7; *Hiya!* magazine profiles with new wife Asti 109–17; in the commentary box 110–11; new Macclesfield dream home 109–17; Peter DeCoursey and 120, 240; Sink the Brown range 113–14
Wilkes, Tiffany 113, 115
William, Prince 130
Williams, Rowan: banjo 21, 24, 28, 34–39, 47, 49, 54–68, 70, 75, 101–104, 112, 116, 124–128, 130, 208, 223–227, 251, 259–267, 289, 309, 311, 113, 129–334, 349–390, 405, 410, 419
Williams, Shirley: Ainsley Harriott impersonation 235; affair with Henry Kissinger 66–68; controversial 'Twix' endorsement 21–22
Williams, Zoe 32
Winslet, Kate 129
Winton, Dale 70
Winston, Robert (Prof.) bullied by Richard Dawkins 340; develops clone army of self 14, 16–17; obsession with vaginas 89, 91
Winstone, Ray: branded perfume range 108–109; love of macramé 54; 'throws like a girl' 212
Wogan, Terry: Home 202
Wogan/Gorbachev (Morgan) 222
Wonder, Stevie 131
Wonnacott, Tim 56, 57
Word Search 188
working-class sitcom, pitch for a 11–15
Wren, Christopher 201
Wytcliff, Connie 21

X

X-Factor, The 71

Y

Yalta Conference, 1945 107
You Know Who Your Mates Are (working-class sitcom) characters 12; Damien Allen's opinion on 14, 15; example programme 13; proposal for 11–15; Tristram Allen's opinion on 14, 15

Z

Zoroastrianism 39

Photo Credits

Julian Humphries: 58, 65, 69, 72, 73, 83, 88, 89, 91, 106, 109, 110, 111, 112, 113, 114, 115, 116, 117, 118, 119, 120, 121, 122, 123, 124, 125, 126, 127, 135, 136, 137, 138, 148, 155, 187, 207, 214, 215, 216, 217, 218, 219, 220, 221, 230, 231, 232, 233, 235, 241.

Rex Features: XXV, 16, 20, 23, 30, 46, 51, 53, 54, 61, 62, 63, 64, 70, 71, 86, 92, 99, 100, 101, 102, 103, 105, 107, 128, 129, 130, 131, 140, 156, 157, 158, 159, 224, 249, 250, 251.

Bea Uhart: 93, 95, 98, 101.

BBC Pictures: 45, 110, 141, 143, 224.

Mark Allan for Whizz Kid 196, 197.

Shutterstock: 18, 19, 23, 55, 65, 66, 67, 95, 134, 147, 172, 173, 203, 205.

PA Archive/PA Photos: 108.

Thanks also to Justine Walker.

✱ANSWERS✱ Count the dots Number of dots: 4,562. Dots Challenge Question 1: Yes, Question 2: 632. Don't go Dotty! Number of dots: 3. Don't go, Dotty! Oh she's gone! Number of dots: Poodle. Pseudacu! Number of dots:‗

262